DOES CAPITAL PUNISHMENT DETER CRIME?

Other Books in the At Issue Series:

DOES CAPITAL PUNISHMENT DETER CRIME?

David L. Bender, *Publisher*
Bruno Leone, *Executive Editor*

Bonnie Szumski, *Editorial Director*
Brenda Stalcup, *Managing Editor*
Scott Barbour, *Senior Editor*

Stephen E. Schonebaum, *Book Editor*

An Opposing Viewpoints® Series

Greenhaven Press, Inc.
San Diego, California

Library of Congress Cataloging-in-Publication Data

Does capital punishment deter crime? / Stephen E. Schonebaum, book editor.
　　p.　　cm. — (At issue) (An opposing viewpoints series)
　　Includes bibliographical references and index.
　　ISBN 1-56510-791-8 (lib. bdg. : alk. paper). — ISBN 1-56510-091-3 (pbk. : alk. paper)
　　1. Capital punishment—United States. 2. Punishment in crime deterrence—United States. I. Schonebaum, Stephen E., 1961–　　. II. Series: At issue (San Diego, Calif.) III. Series: Opposing viewpoints series (Unnumbered)
HV8699.U5D64　　1998
364.66′0973—dc21
　　　　　　　　　　　　　　　　　　　　　　　　98-9752
　　　　　　　　　　　　　　　　　　　　　　　　CIP

© 1998 by Greenhaven Press, Inc., PO Box 289009,
San Diego, CA 92198-9009

Printed in the U.S.A.

Every effort has been made to trace owners of copyrighted material.

DOES CAPITAL PUNISHMENT DETER CRIME?

David L. Bender, *Publisher*
Bruno Leone, *Executive Editor*

Bonnie Szumski, *Editorial Director*
Brenda Stalcup, *Managing Editor*
Scott Barbour, *Senior Editor*

Stephen E. Schonebaum, *Book Editor*

An Opposing Viewpoints® Series

Greenhaven Press, Inc.
San Diego, California

Library of Congress Cataloging-in-Publication Data

Does capital punishment deter crime? / Stephen E. Schonebaum, book editor.
    p.   cm. — (At issue) (An opposing viewpoints series)
    Includes bibliographical references and index.
    ISBN 1-56510-791-8 (lib. bdg. : alk. paper). — ISBN 1-56510-091-3 (pbk. : alk. paper)
    1. Capital punishment—United States. 2. Punishment in crime deterrence—United States. I. Schonebaum, Stephen E., 1961– . II. Series: At issue (San Diego, Calif.) III. Series: Opposing viewpoints series (Unnumbered)
HV8699.U5D64   1998
364.66′0973—dc21   98-9752
                                              CIP

Table of Contents

Introduction

Americans have argued over the death penalty since the early days of the republic. Today, high-profile cases provide frequent opportunities for debate between proponents and opponents of capital punishment. For example, in 1997, Timothy McVeigh was convicted and sentenced to death for the 1993 bombing of the federal building in Oklahoma City, which killed 168 people. The execution of Karla Faye Tucker in 1998 for the pickax murder of two people was the first execution of a woman in Texas since 1863 and the second nationally since 1984. In addition, private concerns Americans have about the effect of violent crime on their neighborhoods and families have led many to decide that the death penalty is an acceptable form of punishment and to support politicians who favor it. Public or private, the debate over the death penalty revolves around three questions: 1) Is capital punishment allowable under the U.S. Constitution? 2) Is it moral? 3) Does it deter crime more than life in prison? The focus of this anthology is on the third question.

According to data collected by the federal government, between 1930 and 1968, 3,859 persons were executed in the United States under civil authority. After 1950, the number of executions consistently declined from 105 in 1951 to 2 in 1967—and to zero from 1968 through 1976—primarily due to legal challenges to the death penalty. These challenges culminated in 1972 when the Supreme Court, in the case of *Furman v. Georgia,* ruled that the death penalty was unconstitutional as practiced at the time. The Court found that the arbitrary application of the sentence by juries violated the Eighth Amendment's ban on cruel and unusual punishment. The 5-4 decision effectively struck down all existing state and federal capital punishment statutes. In response, thirty-five states quickly wrote new capital punishment laws that attempted to meet the requirements for fairness and consistency established by the Court. Within four years, six hundred people had been sentenced to death under the new statutes, though none were executed because states were unsure of the constitutionality of their death penalty legislation. In 1976, the Supreme Court reversed its course and ruled that "the punishment of death does not invariably violate the Constitution." The nearly ten-year moratorium on executions ended in 1977 when Utah executed convicted murderer Gary Gilmore by firing squad; since then more than 350 persons have been put to death. As of 1997, more than 3,200 persons are on death row in thirty-four states (thirty-eight states have capital punishment statutes, but four of them have not imposed sentences). All of these prisoners have been convicted of murder; 98 percent are men.

The United States is the only Western democracy that allows capital punishment, and the sentence has widespread popular and political support. In a 1997 *Time* magazine poll, 74 percent of those surveyed said they favor capital punishment for persons convicted of serious crimes. This number, though, masks the conflicted attitudes Americans have toward the death penalty. The same poll reveals that when Americans are asked whether they think vengeance is a legitimate reason to execute a murderer, 60 percent do not. Additionally, a slight majority (52 percent to 45 percent) do not believe the death penalty deters crime. Most Americans may want killers executed, but a majority are uncomfortable with the two primary reasons for capital punishment—vengeance and deterrence.

Deterrence

The theory of deterrence is based on the idea that the threat of punishment must be severe enough to counter the benefits or pleasures that the criminal would receive from the crime. In addition, the punishment must be administered swiftly so that potential criminals will see a clear cause-and-effect relationship between the crime and the punishment. When punishment deters potential criminals from committing crimes, it is called "general deterrence." Another kind of deterrence, "specific deterrence," refers to the inability of convicted criminals to commit further crimes as a result of their punishment. There is no doubt that capital punishment serves as a specific deterrent: The executed criminal will never kill again. However, experts and others have long debated whether capital punishment is a more effective general deterrent than life in prison.

Social scientists have examined the general deterrent effect of capital punishment since the early twentieth century. Early studies, including those by Thorsten Sellin, took two approaches: Some studies compared homicide rates in states with and without capital punishment; others compared homicide rates for states before or after the reintroduction or abolition of capital punishment. Researchers found that murder rates in neighboring states with and without the death penalty were not significantly different. They also found that homicide rates in states did not increase after the abolishment of the death penalty or decrease after the reinstatement of the sanction. More recent comparative studies have come to the same conclusion, supporting Sellin's contention in 1967 that "the presence of the death penalty in law and practice has no discernible effect as a deterrent to murder."

In the mid-1970s, these results were countered by Isaac Ehrlich, a statistician who, after looking at *national* homicide rates between 1930 and 1970, estimated that each execution deterred between seven and eight homicides. Many researchers have tried to duplicate Ehrlich's results, but most of them have been unsuccessful. It has proven extremely difficult to demonstrate a relationship between executions and crime rates nationwide because of the large number of sociodemographic, legal, and historical variables. Criminologist Frank Zimring has suggested, for example, that the omission of key variables in Ehrlich's studies, including the increased availability of guns and the decline in time served in prison for homicide, calls the results into question. Typically, death penalty opponents claim that Ehrlich's results have been proved invalid, while proponents assert that the results are inconclusive. In the end, social science has been unable to either conclusively support or disprove the theory that capital punishment deters crime.

Common sense

Some proponents of capital punishment maintain that social science is incapable of determining the effectiveness of capital punishment because the data is rough and incomplete and because social science lacks a theory adequate enough to interpret the data. Arguments based on common sense, they contend, are enough to prove that capital punishment is effective.

The most powerful argument for the deterrent effect of the death penalty comes from the commonsense notion that people fear death more than life in prison. "What is feared most deters most," says Ernest van den Haag, a professor at Fordham University and a noted proponent of capital punishment. Once in prison, virtually all convicted murderers seek to avoid execution by appealing to reduce their sentence to life in prison. To van den Haag, this is evidence that the death penalty is feared more, and therefore deters more, than a life sentence. Moreover, he argues that even though social science may not be able to prove conclusively that the death penalty deters murder (at least in statistically significant amounts), capital punishment has surely prevented some murders. Many believe this reason enough to use it.

Proponents of capital punishment also contend that the effects of a death sentence are diluted when the execution is not carried out in a reasonable period of time after sentencing. It currently takes an average of ten years from conviction to execution because prisoners abuse the writ of habeas corpus, which guarantees appeals of sentences and convictions in state criminal cases. Critics contend that this delay eliminates the cause-and-effect relationship between crime and punishment that is necessary if punishment is to deter future crimes. Some argue that if the appeals process were reformed, the deterrent effect of capital punishment would be more evident and provable.

Brutalization theory

Some opponents of the death penalty argue that instead of deterring crime, capital punishment actually increases murder rates because the state, through executions, devalues human life. Over 150 years ago, a Massachusetts state representative, Robert Rantoul, came to this conclusion after looking at the proportion of executions to murders in Massachusetts and several European countries. Over one hundred years later, researchers William Bowers and Glenn Pierce studied homicide records in New York State between 1907 and 1963 and found that the murder rate increased slightly in the months following an execution. To explain this phenomenon, Bowers and Pierce developed what is called brutalization theory, which reasons that state-sanctioned executions brutalize the sensibilities of society, making potential murderers less inhibited.

Many opponents of the death penalty also make the argument that because most murders are unplanned and impulsive, murderers are not deterred by capital punishment. In such an emotional state, they maintain, a murderer is unlikely to think about the distant possibility of execution. As Jesse Jackson explains, "The emotionally charged environment in which these crimes take place do not suggest a coolly calculating murderer weighing his options."

People support or oppose capital punishment for complex, often emotional, reasons. For supporters it can be an issue of public safety or political pragmatism. For opponents it can be a sense of justice or outrage at the inequality in sentencing. Ultimately, capital punishment may be an issue of morality. Although van den Haag believes that the death penalty deters more than other punishments, he would be in favor of capital punishment "on grounds of justice alone." He states: "To me, the life of any innocent victim who might be spared has great value; the life of a convicted murderer does not." For van den Haag and those who share his views, retribution in the form of capital punishment is a morally justifiable and necessary response to some crimes. To others, capital punishment is always immoral. Both sides firmly believe they are right.

The viewpoints in *At Issue: Does Capital Punishment Deter Crime?* introduce the range of opinions on the issue of whether the death penalty deters crime, a debate that will continue for as long as criminals kill and are executed for their crimes.

1

The Death Penalty
Is a Deterrent

George E. Pataki

George E. Pataki is the Republican governor of New York.

The death penalty is a necessary tool to fight and deter crime.
Capital punishment deters crime by causing would-be murderers
to fear arrest and conviction and by preventing convicted murderers from killing again. In recent years, violent crime in New
York has dropped dramatically, due in part to the reinstitution of
the death penalty.

Sept. 1, 1995, marked the end of a long fight for justice in New York
and the beginning of a new era in our state that promises safer communities, fewer victims of crime, and renewed personal freedom. For 22
consecutive years, my predecessors had ignored the urgent calls for justice from our citizens—their repeated and pressing demands for the
death penalty in New York State. Even after the legislature passed a reinstatement of the capital punishment law, it was vetoed for 18 years in
a row. (Twelve of those vetoes came from the pen of former Gov. Mario
Cuomo.)

That was wrong. To fight and deter crime effectively, individuals
must have every tool government can afford them, including the death
penalty. Upon taking office, I immediately began the process of reinstating the death penalty. Two months later, I signed the death penalty into
law for the most heinous and ruthless killers in our society.

Protecting the residents of New York against crime and violence is my
first priority. Indeed, it is the most fundamental duty of government. For
too long, coddling of criminals allowed unacceptable levels of violence to
permeate the streets. They were not subject to swift and certain punishment and, as a result, violent criminal acts were not deterred.

For more than two decades, New York was without the death penalty.
During this time, fear of crime was compounded by the fact that, too often, it largely went unpunished.

Reprinted from George E. Pataki, "Death Penalty Is a Deterrent," *USA Today* magazine, March
1997, by permission of the Society for the Advancement of Education, © 1997.

A dramatic drop in violent crime

No more. In New York, the death penalty has turned the tables on fear and put it back where it belongs—in the hearts of criminals. Within just one year, the death penalty helped produce a dramatic drop in violent crime. Just as important, it has restored New Yorkers' confidence in the justice system because they know their government genuinely is committed to their safety.

Honest, hard-working people share my vision for a safer New York, a place where children can play outside without worry; parents can send their kids to school with peace of mind; people can turn to each other on any street corner, in any subway, at any hour, without casting a suspicious eye; and New York citizens—of all races, religion, and ages—pull together and stand firm against crime.

In short, we are creating a state where law-abiding citizens have unlimited freedom from crime—a state where all can raise a family and follow their dreams in neighborhoods, streets, and schools that are free from the scourge of crime and violence. We've made tremendous progress. Although the death penalty has contributed to that progress, it's just one facet of New York's broad anti-crime strategy.

Other major reforms include substantially increasing the sentences for all violent criminals: eliminating parole eligibility for virtually all repeat violent offenders; barring murderers and sex offenders from participating in work release programs; toughening penalties for perpetrators of domestic violence; notifying communities as to the whereabouts of convicted sex offenders; overturning court-created criminal-friendly loopholes to make it easier to prosecute violent criminals; and allowing juries to impose a sentence of life without parole for killers.

These new laws are working. Since I took office in 1995, violent crime has dropped 23%, assaults are down 22%, and murders have dropped by nearly one-third. New Yorkers now live in safer communities because we finally have begun to create a climate that protects and empowers our citizens, while giving criminals good cause to fear arrest and conviction. I believe this has occurred in part because of the strong signal that the death penalty and our other tough new laws sent to violent criminals and murderers: You will be punished with the full force of the law.

Providing justice and saving lives

Shortly before the death penalty went into effect, I listened to the families of 20 murder victims as they told of their pain. No loved ones should have to go through such a wrenching experience. I never will forget the words of Janice Hunter, whose 27-year-old daughter, Adrien, was stabbed 47 times by serial killer Nathaniel White in 1992. Mrs. Hunter spoke for every family member when she said, "It's a heartache that all parents suffer. I have to go to the cemetery to see my daughter. Nathaniel White's mother goes to jail to see him and I don't think it's fair."

Although no law can bring back Mrs. Hunter's daughter, our laws can and must take every responsible step to prevent others from enduring the heartache suffered by her and her family. Before becoming Governor, I supported the death penalty because of my firm conviction that it would act as a significant deterrent and provide a true measure of justice to murder victims and their loved ones.

I know, as do most New Yorkers, that by restoring the death penalty, we have saved lives. Somebody's mother, somebody's brother, somebody's child is alive today because we were strong enough to be tough enough to care enough to do what was necessary to protect the innocent. Preventing a crime from being committed ultimately is more important than punishing criminals after they have shattered innocent lives.

For too long . . . [criminals] were not subject to swift and certain punishment and, as a result, violent criminal acts were not deterred.

No case illustrates this point more clearly than that of Arthur Shawcross. In 1973, Shawcross, one of New York's most ruthless serial killers, was convicted of the brutal rape and murder of two children in upstate New York. Since the death penalty had been declared unconstitutional, Shawcross was sentenced to prison. After serving just 15 years—an absurd prison term given the crime—he was paroled in 1988. In a horrific 21-month killing spree, Shawcross took 11 more lives. That is 11 innocent people who would be alive today had justice been served 24 years ago; 11 families that would have been spared the pain and agony of losing a loved one.

By reinstating the death penalty, New York has sent a clear message to criminals that the lives of our children are worth more than just a 15-year prison term. Moreover, it has given prosecutors the legal wherewithal to ensure New York State never has another Arthur Shawcross.

Applying the ultimate punishment

Too often, we are confronted with wanton acts of violence that cry out for justice. The World Trade Center bombing and the murderous rampage on the Long Island Rail Road by Colin Ferguson are but two examples. The slaying of a police officer in the line of duty is another. To kill a police officer is to commit an act of war against civilized society.

A person who knowingly commits such a heinous act poses a serious threat to us all, for government cannot protect citizens without doing everything it can to protect those charged with our safety. Police officers put their lives on the line, not knowing whether their next traffic stop or call to duty will be their last.

Under New York's death penalty law, those who murder a police officer; a probation, parole, court, or corrections officer; a judge; or a witness or member of a witness' family can face the death penalty. Someone who murders while already serving life in prison, escaping from prison, or committing other serious felonies can face the death penalty.

Contract killers, serial murderers, those who torture their victims, or those who have murdered before also can be sentenced to death. In determining whether the death penalty should be imposed on anyone convicted of first-degree murder, the bill expressly authorizes juries to hear and consider additional evidence whenever the murder was committed as part of an act of terrorism or by someone with two or more prior serious felony convictions.

New York's death penalty is crafted carefully so that only the most inhuman murderers are eligible for it. Upon the conviction of the defendant, a separate sentencing phase is conducted during which the original jury, or a new jury under special circumstances, weighs the facts of the case.

The jury must consider the defendant's prior criminal history, mental capacity, character, background, state of mind, and the extent of his or her participation in the crime. It then compares this evidence with the facts. For the death penalty to be imposed, the jury must reach a verdict unanimously and beyond a reasonable doubt.

Preventing a crime from being committed ultimately is more important than punishing criminals after they have shattered innocent lives.

Our state lived without adequate protection for 22 years. That is 22 years too long. Now, finally, we have begun to empower New Yorkers with the legal tools they need to make their communities safe.

At the same time, we have put lawless sociopaths like Arthur Shawcross on notice. The time that Shawcross spent in prison was not punishment; it was a mere inconvenience that offered New Yorkers nothing more than a 15-year moratorium from his murderous acts.

Our resolve to end crime is only as strong as the laws we pass to punish criminals. By making the death penalty the law of the land in New York, we have demonstrated that resolve, thus strengthening the promise that our children and future generations will grow up in a state that is free of violence.

The death penalty and the other tough initiatives we have passed are just the beginning of an aggressive and comprehensive plan to reclaim our streets and give New Yorkers back the fundamental freedoms they too often felt had been lost to crime and violence. We will continue to do whatever is necessary to ensure that the lives of New Yorkers are unencumbered by violence, and that is why we will continue to pass laws that give our people unlimited freedom to pursue their hopes and dreams.

2

The Death Penalty Hinders
the Fight Against Crime

Robert M. Morgenthau

Robert M. Morgenthau is the district attorney of Manhattan.

The death penalty is popular among politicians and the public in response to the escalating fear of violence. However, capital punishment actually makes the fight against crime more difficult. Executions waste valuable resources that could be applied to more promising efforts to protect the public. Additionally, innocent people are sometimes executed and the brutalizing effect executions have on society may result in more murders. For these reasons, the death penalty should be opposed.

People concerned about the escalating fear of violence, as I am, may believe that capital punishment is a good way to combat that trend. Take it from someone who has spent a career in Federal and state law enforcement, enacting the death penalty in New York State would be a grave mistake.

Prosecutors must reveal the dirty little secret they too often share only among themselves: The death penalty actually hinders the fight against crime.

Promoted by members of both political parties in response to an angry populace, capital punishment is a mirage that distracts society from more fruitful, less facile answers. It exacts a terrible price in dollars, lives and human decency. Rather than tamping down the flames of violence, it fuels them while draining millions of dollars from more promising efforts to restore safety to our lives.

Not a deterrent

Even proponents have been forced to concede that more than a century's experience has not produced credible evidence that executions deter crime. That's why many district attorneys throughout New York State and America oppose it—privately. Fear of political repercussions keeps them from saying so publicly.

To deter crime, punishment must be prompt and certain. Resources should be focused on that goal and on recidivists and career criminals, who commit a disproportionate share of all crime, including murder.

In 1994, 6,100 criminals were sentenced to state prison in Manhattan, and 9,000 more were sent to city jail. That is the constructive way to be tough on crime. In 1975, when I became District Attorney, there were 648 homicides in Manhattan; in 1994, there were 330. The number has been cut virtually in half without executions—proof to me that they are not needed to continue that trend.

Many district attorneys throughout New York State and America oppose [capital punishment]—privately.

Executions waste scarce law-enforcement financial and personnel resources. An authoritative study by Duke University in 1993 found that for each person executed in North Carolina, the state paid over $2 million more than it would have cost to imprison him for life, in part because of court proceedings.

In New York, the cost would be higher. A 1989 study by the Department of Correctional Services estimated that the death penalty would cost the state $118 million a year. More crime would be prevented if a fraction of that money were spent on an array of solutions from prisons to drug treatment programs.

Executing the innocent

If you have the death penalty, you will execute innocent people. No one disagrees that such horrors occur—the only argument concerns how often. A 1987 study in the *Stanford Law Review* identified 350 cases in this century in which innocent people were wrongly convicted of crimes for which they could have received the death penalty; of that number, perhaps as many as 23 were executed. New York led the list with eight.

In 1995, an appalling miscarriage of justice occurred when Texas executed Jesse DeWayne Jacobs. He was sentenced to death for a murder he originally confessed to—but later claimed had been committed by his sister. In the subsequent trial of his sister, the prosecutor unequivocally disavowed the confession he had used to convict Mr. Jacobs. He argued that Mr. Jacobs had told the truth when he said that his sister had pulled the trigger and that he had not anticipated any murder. Mr. Jacobs was executed anyway.

Some crimes are so depraved that execution might seem just. But even in the impossible event that a statute could be written and applied so wisely that it would reach only those cases, the price would still be too high.

It has long been argued, with statistical support, that by their brutalizing and dehumanizing effect on society, executions cause more murders than they prevent. "After every instance in which the law violates the sanctity of human life, that life is held less sacred by the community among whom the outrage is perpetrated." Those words written in 1846 by Robert Rantoul Jr., a Massachusetts legislator, are no less true today.

Murders like those at the Brookline, Mass., abortion clinics in 1994 are monstrous even if a killer believes his cause is just. Yet when the state kills, it sends the opposite message: the death penalty endorses violent solutions, and violence begets violence.

The only honest justification for the death penalty is vengeance, but the Lord says, "Vengeance is mine." It is wrong for secular governments to try to usurp that role. That's why New York should reject the death penalty.

[Editor's note: Morgenthau wrote this opinion piece to oppose the campaign to restore capital punishment in New York State. The bid to bring back the death penalty to New York succeeded, and on September 1, 1995, the punishment was reinstated.]

3

A Swifter Death Penalty Would Be an Effective Deterrent

Arlen Specter

Arlen Specter is a Republican senator from Pennsylvania.

The writ of habeas corpus, which is intended to protect the rights of defendants by allowing them to appeal their convictions and sentences for federal judicial review, is being used to delay death sentences. The abuse of this safeguard causes unnecessary delays (on average, nine years) that diminish the deterrent effect of the death penalty. This delay in executions results in a miscarriage of justice for both crime victims and defendants.

The American people want government to do something about violent crime. Unfortunately, it is now almost certain that whatever crime legislation we pass in 1994 will do nothing about one of the most serious aspects of the crime problem: the interminable appeals process that has made the death penalty more a hollow threat than an effective deterrent.

Both the House and Senate versions of the 1994 crime bill abandoned key provisions that would limit appeals in the federal courts by state death-row inmates. These appeals currently average nine years and last as long as seventeen years, which precludes the death penalty from being an effective deterrent. National polls now show fear of crime to be the No. 1 concern of most Americans. One survey conducted right after President Clinton's 1994 State of the Union Address found that 71% of respondents thought more murders should be punishable by the death penalty.

The importance of habeas corpus

The great writ of habeas corpus has been the procedure used to guarantee defendants in state criminal trials their rights under the U.S. Constitution. It is an indispensable safeguard because of the documented history of state criminal-court abuses like the 1931 Scottsboro case [in which nine

Reprinted, with permission, from Arlen Specter, "Congress Must Make Death Sentences Meaningful Again," *Human Events*, July 15, 1995.

black teenagers were accused of raping two white women and sentenced to death. They were later acquitted]. Unfortunately, it has been applied in a crazy-quilt manner with virtually endless appeals that deny justice to victims and defendants alike, making a mockery of the judicial system.

This incredibly complicated legal process must be understood by the public if sufficient pressure is to be put on Congress to correct this egregious problem.

Delays leave inmates, as well as victims, in a difficult state of suspended animation. In a 1989 case, the British government declined to extradite a defendant to Virginia on murder charges until the death penalty was dropped, because the European Court of Human Rights had ruled that confinement in a Virginia prison for six to eight years awaiting execution violated the European Convention on Human Rights.

Similarly, for survivors of murder victims, there is an inability to reach a sense of resolution concerning their loved one's death until the criminal case has been resolved. The families do not understand the complexities of the legal process and experience feelings of isolation, anger and loss of control over the lengthy court proceedings. The unconscionable delays deny justice to all—society, victims and defendants.

Since it upheld the constitutionality of the death penalty in 1976, the U.S. Supreme Court has required more clearly defined death penalty laws. Thirty-seven [thirty-eight as of 1998] state legislatures have responded to the voters' expressions of public outrage by enacting capital punishment statutes that meet the requirements of the Constitution.

The death penalty is a deterrent

My twelve years' experience in the Philadelphia District Attorney's Office convinced me that the death penalty is a deterrent to crime. I saw many cases where professional burglars and robbers refused to carry weapons for fear that a killing would occur and they would be charged with murder in the first degree, carrying the death penalty.

One such case involved three hoodlums who planned to rob a Philadelphia pharmacist. Cater, 19, and Rivers, 18, saw that their partner Williams, 20, was carrying a revolver. The two younger men said they would not participate if Williams took the revolver along, so Williams placed the gun in a drawer and slammed it shut.

Right as the three men were leaving the room, Williams sneaked the revolver back into his pocket. In the course of the robbery, pharmacist Jacob Viner was shot to death by Williams. The details of the crime emerged from the confessions of the three defendants and corroborating evidence. All three men were sentenced to the death penalty, because under the law, Cater and Rivers were equally responsible for Williams' act of murder.

Ultimately Williams was executed and the death penalties for Cater and Rivers were changed to life imprisonment because of extenuating circumstances, since they did not know a weapon was being carried by their co-conspirator. There are many, many similar cases, where robbers and burglars avoid carrying weapons for fear a gun or knife will be used in a murder, subjecting them to the death penalty.

The use of the death penalty has gradually been limited by the courts and legislatures to apply only to the most outrageous cases. In 1925, the

Pennsylvania Legislature repealed the mandatory death penalty for first-degree murder, leaving it to the discretion of the jury or trial court. More recently, in 1972, the Supreme Court struck down all state and federal death-penalty laws and prohibited capital punishment for all inmates on death row, or future executions, unless thereafter they contained detailed procedures for consideration of aggravating and mitigating circumstances.

The unconscionable delays deny justice to all—society, victims and defendants.

Prosecutors customarily refrain from asking for the death penalty in all but the most heinous crimes. I did that when I was a district attorney—personally reviewing the cases where capital punishment was requested.

While the changes required by the Supreme Court help insure justice to defendants, there is a sense that capital punishment can be retained only if applied in outrageous cases. I agree with advocates who insist on the greatest degree of care in the use of capital punishment and have voted for limitations to exclude the death penalty for the mentally impaired and the very young. However, I oppose those who search for every possible excuse to avoid the death penalty because they oppose it on the grounds of conscientious scruples.

While I understand and respect that moral opposition, our system of government says the people of the thirty-seven states that have capital punishment are entitled to have those sentences carried out where it has been constitutionally imposed. In those jurisdictions, the debate is over until the statutes have been repealed or the Constitution re-interpreted.

Abuse of the appeals process

Many federal habeas corpus appeals demonstrate virtually endless delays, where judges bounce capital cases like tennis balls from one court to another. Here is an example. After being convicted in California for a double murder in 1980, Robert Alton Harris filed ten petitions for habeas corpus review in the state courts, five similar petitions in the federal courts and eleven applications to the Supreme Court of the United States. Many of those applications to invalidate his death penalty overlapped.

The absurdity of these proceedings is illustrated by the series of decisions involving a Philadelphia criminal, Michael Peoples, who was convicted in the state trial court on charges of robbery and setting the victim on fire. Following this legal trial is not easy, but it is illustrative of the farcical procedures. After the Pennsylvania intermediate appellate court affirmed his conviction, the Pennsylvania Supreme Court denied review in a decision that was unclear whether it was based on the merits or the court's procedural discretion that there was no special reason to consider the substantive issues.

Peoples then filed a petition for habeas corpus in the United States District Court that was denied for failure to exhaust state remedies—meaning the state court did not consider all his claims. The case was then appealed to the next higher court level, the Third Circuit Court of Appeals, which reversed the District Court on the ground that the exhaustion rule was satisfied when the state supreme court had the opportunity to correct alleged violations of the prisoner's constitutional rights. Next, the defendant asked the Supreme Court of the United States to review his case.

Even though the Supreme Court was too busy to hear 4,550 cases that year, the Peoples case was one of the 147 petitions it granted. After the nine justices reviewed the briefs, heard oral argument and deliberated, Justice Antonin Scalia wrote an opinion reversing the Court of Appeals for the Third Circuit.

The Third Circuit then undertook the extensive process of briefs and argument before three judges. It issued a complicated opinion concluding that the original petition for a writ of habeas corpus contained both exhausted and unexhausted claims. That ruling sent the case back to the District Court for reconsideration. This is the short version of what happened in those six courts.

The need to speed up the process

Had the District Court simply considered the defendant's constitutional claims on the substantive merits in the first instance, all those briefs, arguments and opinions would have been avoided. These complications arise from a federal statute that requires a defendant to exhaust his or her remedies in the state court before coming to the federal court. The original purpose of giving the state a chance to correct any error and to limit the work of the federal courts was sound. In practice, however, that rule has created a hopeless maze, illustrated by thousands of cases like Peoples and Harris.

The elimination of the statutory exhaustion requirement would mean that Congress, which has authority to establish federal court jurisdiction, would direct United States district courts to decide petitions for writs of habeas corpus after direct appeals to the Supreme Court had upheld the death penalty. From my own experience, I have seen state trial court judges sit on such habeas corpus cases for months or years and then dismiss them in the most perfunctory way because the issues had already been decided by the state supreme court in its earlier decision.

> *I oppose those who search for every possible excuse to avoid the death penalty because they oppose it on the grounds of conscientious scruples.*

Unless there are unusually complicating factors, which have to be detailed in the district court's opinion, I know that such cases can be heard within two weeks, with no more than a week or two being required to write an opinion. Some district courts have sat on such cases for as long as twelve years. A 180-day time limit would require judges to give priority attention to capital cases.

Even in states with the most prisoners on death row, like Florida, Texas or California, each district court judge would only have such a case every twelve, twenty-five and thirty-six months, respectively.

Decisions on appeals to the courts of appeals should be made within 180 days. That is manageable with priority attention to these relatively few capital cases. The authority of Congress to establish such time limits was exercised in the Speedy Trial Act of 1974, which calls for criminal trials to be concluded within ninety days unless delayed by specified causes.

Eliminating trivial procedural delays

Significant delays on habeas corpus proceedings are caused by successive petitions to district courts, delays in those courts and repetitive appeals to the courts of appeals. Reform should require permission from a panel of three court of appeals' judges before a successive petition may be filed. This approach would preclude numerous, successive federal habeas corpus petitions like the five filed by Robert Harris in the fourteen-year California case. The successive petition would be permitted only if the facts could not have been previously discovered through reasonable diligence, the claim is based on a new rule, or state officials caused the claim not to be raised earlier.

Obviously, federal habeas corpus is a complex and arcane subject. Its difficult and restrictive rules simply delay imposition of the death penalty and render it meaningless as a deterrent. The purposes of tough law enforcement are best served by full hearings, even in retroactive issues, instead of allowing the procedural morass to defeat the substantive benefits of capital punishment. Practical reinstatement of the death penalty by habeas corpus reform is well worth pursuing, so that meaningless procedures do not remain the enemy of substantive justice.

4

The Death Penalty Is Not an Effective Law Enforcement Tool

Richard C. Dieter

Richard C. Dieter is a lawyer and executive director of the Death Penalty Information Center, an anti–capital punishment advocacy group.

In a nationwide poll, a group of randomly selected police chiefs were asked what they believe really works in fighting crime and whether the death penalty is an effective crime-fighting tool. While many of the chiefs support the death penalty philosophically, a strong majority do not believe that it is an effective law enforcement tool in practice. Police chiefs view other methods of controlling crime as more effective, including gun control, community policing, neighborhood crime programs, and more vigilant efforts against drug crime and youth crime. Additionally, chiefs rank capital punishment as less cost-effective than other methods available to them, and a vast majority do not believe that the threat of the death penalty deters murderers from committing homicide.

I think that the only purpose for the death penalty, as I see it, is vengeance— pure and simple vengeance. But I think vengeance is a very personal feeling and I don't think it is something that civilized government should engage in.

—Janet Reno, Attorney General of the United States[1]

The death penalty does little to prevent crime. It's the fear of apprehension and the likely prospect of swift and certain punishment that provides the largest deterrent to crime.

—Frank Friel, Former Head of Organized Crime Homicide Task Force, Philadelphia[2]

Take it from someone who has spent a career in Federal and state law enforcement, enacting the death penalty . . . would be a grave mistake. Prosecutors must reveal the dirty little secret they too often share only among themselves: The death penalty actually hinders the fight against crime.

—Robert M. Morgenthau, District Attorney, Manhattan, NY[3]

Reprinted from Richard C. Dieter, "On the Front Line: Law Enforcement Views on the Death Penalty," a publication of the Death Penalty Information Center, Washington, D.C., February 1995, by permission of the author.

I am not convinced that capital punishment, in and of itself, is a deterrent to crime because most people do not think about the death penalty before they commit a violent or capital crime.
                    —Willie L. Williams, Former Police Chief, Los Angeles, CA[4]

A new national survey of police chiefs from around the country discredits the repeated assertion that the death penalty is an important law enforcement tool. While politicians have extolled the importance of capital punishment in fighting crime, they have failed to assess the actual priorities of those in law enforcement and have saddled the taxpayers with an enormously costly death penalty at the expense of more effective crime fighting strategies.

In January, 1995, Peter D. Hart Research Associates conducted a national opinion poll of randomly selected police chiefs in the United States. In that poll, the chiefs had the opportunity to express what they believe really works in fighting crime. They were asked where the death penalty fit in their priorities as leaders in the law enforcement field. What the police chiefs had to say may be surprising to many lawmakers, and to much of the public as well. The Hart Poll found that:

- Police chiefs rank the death penalty *last* as a way of reducing violent crime, placing it behind curbing drug abuse, more police officers on the streets, lowering the technical barriers to prosecution, longer sentences, and a better economy with more jobs.
- The death penalty was rated as the *least cost-effective* method for controlling crime.
- Insufficient use of the death penalty is *not* considered a major problem by the majority of police chiefs.
- Strengthening families and neighborhoods, punishing criminals swiftly and surely, controlling illegal drugs, and gun control are considered much more important than the death penalty.
- Although a majority of the police chiefs support the death penalty in the abstract, when given a choice between the sentence of life without parole plus restitution versus the death penalty, *barely half of the chiefs support capital punishment.*
- Police chiefs *do not believe* that the death penalty significantly *reduces the number of homicides.*
- Police chiefs *do not believe that murderers think about the range of possible punishments.*
- Debates about the death penalty *distract Congress and state legislatures from focusing on real solutions to crime.*

In sum, while many police chiefs support the death penalty philosophically, a strong majority do not believe that it is an effective law enforcement tool in practice. In the report below, the various findings of this poll will be explored in depth, along with a broader analysis of what really works in reducing crime. The results of this opinion poll are confirmed by the statements of individual leaders in the law enforcement community, by research in the field of criminology, and by the recommendations of many of the nation's leading law enforcement agencies.

A national poll

In 1994, crime was the nation's number one concern. Despite political gridlock on many other issues, President Clinton was able to move a $30 billion crime bill through Congress, including a major expansion of the federal death penalty. The elections in November produced a cascade of candidates tripping over each other to sound even tougher than their opponent on crime. Campaign advertisements reached new lows in mongering fear in the electorate in order to boost the chances of "law and order" politicians. Candidates used the death penalty as a club, even against those who supported it.

But few, if any, politicians took the time to ask those in law enforcement what they thought would really work in preventing crime. Was the death penalty, in fact, the top priority for law enforcement that it was for the politicians?

Police views on crime prevention

Law enforcement officers are society's front line in fighting crime. They see it up close every day, and they have a personal stake in reducing violence. So, it is natural to ask them: "What, in your opinion, works in the battle against crime?"

This question was approached from a variety of directions. Police were first given an open-ended opportunity to state the areas that would have the biggest impact on reducing violent crime in their jurisdiction. Sentencing reform, including truth in sentencing, elimination of parole and stiffer sentences was the most often cited area of reform (33% of respondents). Other areas of emphasis included the development of family values and parenting skills (23%), education (15%), and more police (13%). The death penalty was mentioned by fewer than 2% of the chiefs and followed twenty-five other areas of concern.

The police chiefs were also asked to select their primary choices from a list of possible ways to reduce violent crime. The need to reduce the prevalence of drug abuse was their first priority. They also chose longer prison sentences for criminals, fewer technical legal barriers to the prosecution of criminals, more police officers on the street, a better economy with more jobs, and reducing the number of guns over an expanded use of the death penalty as better ways to lower crime. Capital punishment ranked a distant last, with only 1% of the chiefs citing it as their primary focus for stopping violent crime. These results are illustrated in Figure 1.

In a similar vein, the poll explored what the police chiefs see as the main obstacles to their success as they try to protect citizens and fashion a safer society. Again, drug and alcohol abuse surfaced as the most frequently mentioned problem facing police forces today. Fully 87% chose this as a serious problem (i.e., "top two or three problems" or as a "major problem") which they encounter in their work. Family problems or child abuse was the second major obstacle for police, with 77% citing this as a serious problem in their jurisdiction.

The police chiefs were evenly split between those stating that a lack of law enforcement resources was a serious problem (49%) and those who thought it was at most a minor problem (50%). About 45% of the police

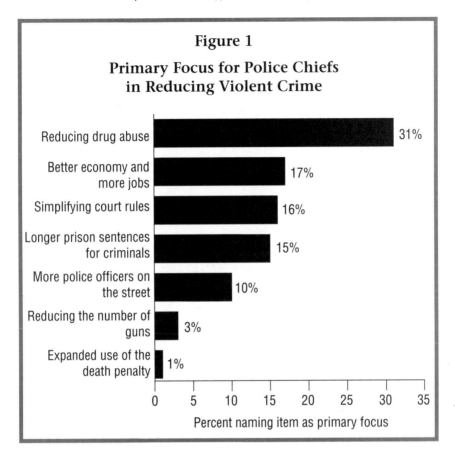

Figure 1

Primary Focus for Police Chiefs in Reducing Violent Crime

chiefs stated that the availability of too many guns was a serious problem. Interestingly, most of the chiefs did not see gangs as a major problem in their efforts. Only 7% reported that gangs were one of their top two or three problems.

Other areas which were cited as major problems included crowded courts and slow justice. On the other hand, ineffective prosecution and high unemployment were only rated as minor problems. Again, the death penalty ranked near the bottom as a serious concern for law enforcement officers. Insufficient use of the death penalty was rated as either a minor problem or no problem at all by 63% of the respondents. (See Figure 2.)

No one is more keenly aware of the fact that preventing crime costs money than police chiefs. Faced daily with budget decisions and the rising costs of salaries, training and equipment for a police force, chiefs must constantly balance emergency responses and long-term needs. The Hart Poll sought to discover not only what police chiefs ideally want in the fight against crime, but also what are the most cost-effective methods available to them.

Among strategies used for controlling crime, the death penalty ranked *last* in terms of its cost-effectiveness. The related areas of community policing and expanded training with more equipment for police received the highest cost-effective ratings by the police chiefs among ways to reduce crime. Fifty-six percent of the respondents rated these areas as cost-effective (i.e., they gave it an 8, 9, or 10 out of a possible 10). Imposing the death penalty more often was thought to be cost-effective by only 29% of the chiefs. Neighborhood watch programs ranked almost as high as community policing in terms of effectiveness for the dollars spent. Figure 3 illustrates the relative cost-effectiveness which the police gave to these various measures.

Reliable estimates indicate that the cost of the death penalty to taxpayers is over $2 million per execution, with the bulk of the costs occurring at the trial level.[5] That figure is a measure of the *extra* costs attributable solely to capital punishment, beyond the costs of a typical murder case without the death penalty and the costs of incarceration resulting from a life sentence.

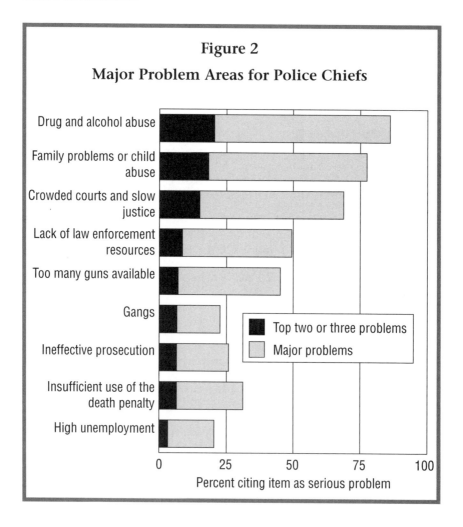

Figure 2

Major Problem Areas for Police Chiefs

There are increasing demands for the limited crime fighting resources. Many states and counties are strapped for funds and are facing severe budget crises. Hard choices have to be made among various strategies for fighting crime. If $2 million is spent on the death penalty, then that same money is not available for more police officers, or for bulletproof vests, or for speedier trials, or neighborhood watch programs, or community policing.

It currently costs three times as much—more than $2 million per inmate—to carry out the death sentence than to keep an inmate in prison for 40 years.
—Former Texas Attorney General, Jim Mattox[6]

The average salary for a new police officer is about $42,000 per year, including benefits.[7] Thus, $2 million translates into approximately 48 additional police officers, a far more likely and immediate deterrent to crime than one remote execution. Similarly, the same $2 million could buy thousands of bullet-proof vests, or provide improved lighting in high-crime areas, or could be used as seed money for neighborhood watch programs.

Community policing

In the survey, police chiefs voiced their support for more police on the streets, and for community policing in particular, as an effective way of fighting crime. The value of community policing is confirmed by success stories from various communities. Community policing has been cited by a number of cities as the chief reason why they have experienced a reduction in crime.

Community policing was introduced in New York City in 1990 and for four years since then crime has gone down in virtually every category.[8] Boston, too, cited the expansion of its police force as one reason for its drop in crime.[9] In Fort Worth, Texas, crime dropped by 24 percent in 1993 to its lowest level in ten years. Police cited the department's involvement in the Justice Department's "Weed and Seed" program, employing a combination of drug interdiction and social programs in targeted areas. They also added 55 officers designated as neighborhood patrol officers and utilized 1,500 community residents in a "Citizens on Patrol" program.[10]

In San Jose, California, community policing was credited with an 11 percent drop in crime.[11] In Prince George's County, Maryland, police Capt. Terry Evans described community policing as, "the only thing I've seen in 23 years of law enforcement that's had an impact, actually turned it around."[12]

Lee P. Brown, former N.Y. City Police Commissioner, stressed the preventive power of community policing: "I can assure you that in the end the community police officer permanently assigned to the neighborhood is a better deterrent to unrest than a SWAT team waiting in the wings."[13]

In another survey of police officers, this one focusing on officers in Texas and California, Dr. Joseph Zelan found that 78 percent of police

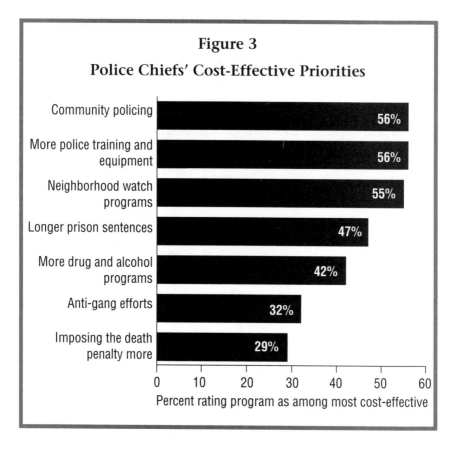

Figure 3

Police Chiefs' Cost-Effective Priorities

Percent rating program as among most cost-effective

officers viewed community policing as positive, and only 1 percent of the respondents were very negative about it. Almost 60 percent of those surveyed believed that community policing would reduce crime rates.[14]

Deterring crime

One of the principal reasons that those in law enforcement are not enamored of the death penalty is that they do not believe it is a deterrent to crime. Law enforcement officers believe that the most effective deterrent to crime is swift and sure punishment. When asked which societal or legal changes would have the greatest impact on reducing violent crime, police chose strengthening families and neighborhoods, along with swift and sure punishment for offenders, as the means that would bring about the most significant effects.

Police wanted more control over illicit drugs, greater latitude for judges in criminal cases, greater economic opportunity, and a reduction in the number of guns in circulation. Expanding the death penalty, on the other hand, was not thought to have a big impact on crime reduction.

Over two-thirds of the police chiefs did not believe that the death penalty significantly reduces the number of homicides. About 67% said

Figure 4

Dispelling the Myths About the Usefulness of the Death Penalty

Myth I: Murderers think about possible punishments

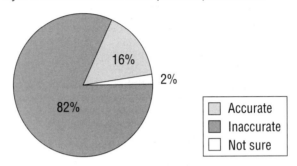

Myth II: Death penalty significantly reduces number of homicides

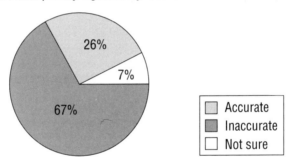

Myth III: Death penalty is one of most important tools

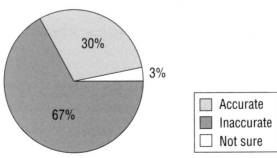

that it was not one of the most important law enforcement tools. And well over 80% of the respondents believe that murderers do not think about the range of possible punishments before committing homicide. Figure 4 illustrates the lack of confidence which police chiefs place in the death penalty as a deterrent.

One of the many problems with the death penalty is that it is anything but swift and sure. Even under current proposals for restricting death penalty appeals, the sentence would be carried out years after it is imposed, on relatively few of all the convicted murderers, and with a substantial likelihood that the sentence will be overturned before the execution is carried out. Sentences of life without parole, in contrast, begin immediately upon sentencing and are rarely overturned on appeal.

Capital cases are a nightmare for the entire justice system. Police chiefs recognize that death penalty cases are particularly burdensome in the early stages. Two-thirds of the police chiefs polled said that death penalty cases are hard to close and take up a lot of police time.

Jim Mattox, former Attorney General of Texas, who supported the death penalty during his term of office and oversaw many of the state's first executions after the death penalty was reinstated, does not believe that murderers in Texas are deterred by the death penalty. Mattox interviewed nearly all the people executed in Texas between 1976 and 1988 and concluded that the sentence of death never crossed their minds before their crime[15]: "It is my own experience that those executed in Texas were not deterred by the existence of the death penalty," he said. "I think in most cases you'll find that the murder was committed under severe drug and alcohol abuse."[16]

Lieutenant Gregory Ruff, a police officer in Kansas for 23 years, agrees: "I have seen the ugliness of murder up close and personal. But I have never heard a murder suspect say they thought about the death penalty as a consequence of their actions prior to committing their crimes."[17]

Willie Williams, Chief of Police in Los Angeles, echoed the same theme from his years of experience: "I am not convinced that capital punishment, in and of itself, is a deterrent to crime because most people do not think about the death penalty before they commit a violent or capital crime."[18]

Another reason why the death penalty fails as a law enforcement tool is that one of the most violent segments of the population is the least likely to be deterred by prospective punishments. Many who might face the death penalty live in a culture of violence. The leading cause of death among young black men, for example, is murder.[19] They are more likely to be killed by a rival gang member or by a drug dealer whom they double-crossed than by the state. James Fox, dean of the College of Criminal Justice at Northeastern University, has noted the fast growth in violent crime among teenagers: "Many of them face death every day of their lives. They don't think about the possibility—as remote as it is—that they'll someday die for a crime. These kids are all armed and in gangs, and they worry about dying next week."[20] In such an environment, the threat of the death penalty adds little to the danger.

The Hart survey showed that police chiefs are very much aware of the problems among youth today. Strengthening families, neighborhoods and churches were among their top priorities throughout the poll. In the open-ended question about changes which would most likely reduce violent crime, police mentioned concerns about the needs of young people and juvenile offenders ahead of a desire for more police or financial resources.

Richard H. Girgenti, the New York State Director of Criminal Justice, noted that "[d]emographics have always been the best predictor of future crime." [21] In preparing for challenges in combating crime in the next decade, it is sobering to note that murders by those between the ages of 14 to 17 grew by 124% between 1986 and 1991, while murder among adults 25 and over actually declined. [22] Since many teenagers are not even legally eligible for the death penalty, much less deterred by it, and since the number of teenagers in the population will be growing tremendously in the next 10 years, more creative approaches to preventing violent crime are essential.

Even when it comes to the killing of a police officer, the death penalty is not a deterrent. Texas, by far the leading death penalty state, for the past six years has also been the leading state in the number of its police officers killed. By comparison, in 1994 New York, with no death penalty, had about one-third as many officers killed as Texas. [23]

A recent study of the deterrence value of the death penalty published in the *Journal of Social Issues* surveyed a 13-year period of police homicides. The researchers concluded: "[W]e find no consistent evidence that capital punishment influenced police killings during the 1976–1989 period. . . . [P]olice do not appear to have been afforded an added measure of protection against homicide by capital punishment." [24]

In a nation with over 200 million firearms, gun control is also a priority among many law enforcement agencies. About 45% of police chiefs listed the easy availability of guns as a major problem in fighting crime, though only 38% thought that reducing the number of guns would have a big impact on crime. The International Association of Chiefs of Police, the largest such organization in the world, called for strict control of certain weapons: "The deadly flow of military assault-type automatic and semiautomatic weapons onto the streets of America and into the hands of violent criminals means that all too frequently the superior firepower belongs to the criminals, not law enforcement." [25] They called for a complete ban: "Manufacture and sale of assault weapons to the general public should be prohibited." [26] Other police organizations have also supported tighter gun controls. [27]

Many politicians say the death penalty would help us in New York by deterring would-be killers. I believe it would make things worse because it is another instruction in brutality.
—Thomas A. Coughlin III, former commissioner, New York State Dept. of Correctional Services [28]

While the public is deeply concerned about violent crime, it is really gun-related crime that has shown the most dramatic increases. According to the FBI, the violent crime rate has actually decreased over the past decade, but crimes with handguns have grown disturbingly. From 1987 to 1992, handgun crimes rose 55 percent.[29]

A comparison of handgun deaths in the United States as contrasted with other countries demonstrates how serious a problem guns are. In 1992, the United States suffered 13,220 murders by handguns. By comparison, there were only 128 such deaths in Canada, 60 in Japan, only 33 in Great Britain, and just 13 in Australia.[30] Some experts in European countries attribute their lower murder rates to stricter gun controls.[31]

We may have put the caboose on the front—we should have gone after guns first. . . . Decent folk are just tired of living under the threat of the gun.
—James D. Toler, Chief of Police,
Kansas City, Missouri[32]

A recent profile of the criminal justice systems in the United States and England published by the U.S. Department of Justice highlighted other interesting differences between these two countries. Violent crime was significantly higher in the U.S., with the homicide rate in the U.S. being almost seven times that in England and Wales. England and Wales employed proportionately more law enforcement officers (256 per 100,000 population) than did the U.S. (240 officers per 100,000 population), and spent more per resident on their justice system than did the U.S.[33] None of that spending went toward the death penalty, which has been abolished in the United Kingdom.

Support for the death penalty

A clear majority of the police chiefs in the Hart Poll say that capital punishment is not an effective law enforcement tool, even though they support it philosophically. The chiefs were asked which of three statements came closest to their own point of view:

- I support the death penalty and think it works well.
- Philosophically, I support the death penalty, but I don't think it is an effective law enforcement tool in practice.
- I oppose the death penalty.

About a third of the respondents approved of the death penalty in practice. On the other hand, 58% of the police chiefs, while supporting the death penalty philosophically, did not think it was an effective law enforcement tool. When combined with the percentage who opposed capital punishment completely, this result corresponded well with the two-thirds of police chiefs who disagreed that the death penalty significantly reduces the number of homicides and the equal number who say that murderers do not think about the range of punishments before committing homicides. (See Figure 5.)

Police chiefs recognize that the death penalty has been overused by politicians. Ronald Hampton, President of the National Black Police

Association in Washington, DC, noted: "[The death penalty] is a political move, insensitive to the real needs of the people in this city."[34] Eighty-five percent of the chiefs polled believed that politicians support the death penalty as a symbolic way to show they are tough on crime. In line with their belief that capital punishment is not an important law enforcement tool, the majority of police chiefs believed that time spent on capital punishment in Congress and in state legislatures distracts from finding real solutions to the problems of crime.

Similar to the results of recent opinion polls showing the public's openness to death penalty alternatives,[35] the Hart Poll showed that police chiefs believe in harsh punishment for those who commit murder, though, not necessarily, the death penalty. When offered the alternative sentence of life imprisonment with no possibility of parole, combined with mandatory restitution to the victim's family, support for the death penalty among police chiefs drops to only 50%. And among the majority of police chiefs who do not believe the death penalty is effective in practice, 52% would prefer the alternative sentence over capital punishment.

Proposals for fighting crime

Many organizations in the United States are committed to law enforcement and to finding solutions to the problems of crime and violence. In grappling with these issues, a number of these organizations have produced statements and studies on what can be done to reduce crime. The proposed solutions range from a fundamental restructuring of society to more immediate innovations that citizens can implement in their own neighborhoods. Rarely is the death penalty even mentioned in their discussions. Instead, the solutions are changes and programs that affect a broad range of people and go to the roots of why violent crime has become so prevalent.

I have never heard a murder suspect say they thought about the death penalty as a consequence of their actions prior to committing their crimes.
—Police Lieut. Gregory Ruff, Kansas

Because the root causes of violence are so deeply entrenched and so difficult to change, the death penalty presents a tempting "quick fix" to a complex problem. Nevertheless, many law enforcement groups have taken crime head-on and have proposed a variety of practical remedies.

In *A National Action Plan to Combat Violent Crime,* police chiefs from Atlanta, Boston, Louisville, Knoxville, Salt Lake City, Chicago, and Washington, DC, along with the U.S. Conference of Mayors, teamed together in 1993 to address the crime emergency and to make recommendations to the President of the United States. Their crime fighting priorities reflect many of the same concerns which were voiced by police chiefs all over the country in the Hart Poll:

1. *Funds for additional police officers,* and the implementation of community policing, with no cut in other programs that address urban needs and the root causes of crime.

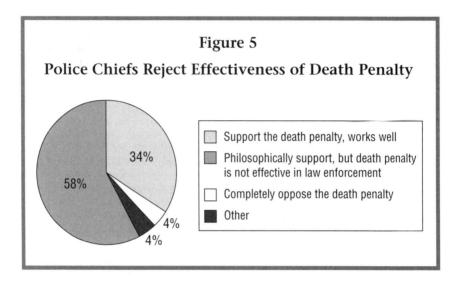

Figure 5

Police Chiefs Reject Effectiveness of Death Penalty

34%

58%

4%

4%

☐ Support the death penalty, works well

▨ Philosophically support, but death penalty is not effective in law enforcement

☐ Completely oppose the death penalty

■ Other

2. *Omnibus firearm control measures,* including:
   - Banning the manufacture, sale and possession of all semiautomatic assault weapons and their component parts
   - Registration of all newly purchased and transferred firearms
   - Expansion of the Brady Law to all firearms sales
   - Liability of gun dealers for damages resulting from illegal sales.
3. *Expanded drug control efforts,* including:
   - Expansion of treatment programs so that services are available to all in need
   - Mandatory minimum sentences for all repeat drug sale convictions
   - Establishment of additional drug courts.
4. *Restructuring and strengthening the criminal justice system,* including:
   - Emphasis on juvenile crime; greater prosecution of violent juvenile offenders as adults
   - Expansion of number of prosecutors, court services and personnel
   - Expansion of boot camps and other alternatives to prisons.
5. *Long-term crime reduction strategy:*
   - Reduce unemployment
   - Community involvement in preventing crime
   - Focus on young people: addressing family violence, jobs, preventing school dropouts
   - Expansion of violence reduction and conflict resolution programs.
6. *Partnerships to prevent violent crime:*
   - More coordination of efforts among mayors, police chiefs and the federal leaders
   - Improved sharing of intelligence and technologies
   - Involvement of schools, public health departments, human service agencies, businesses and neighborhood organizations in crime prevention
   - Confronting the entertainment industry on the proliferation of violence.[36]

The International Association of Chiefs of Police (IACP) also issued a series of recommendations in 1993 in response to the problem of violent crime in America. The IACP convened a summit of police executives from around the country. Participants included representatives of the Bureau of Alcohol, Tobacco, and Firearms, the Federal Bureau of Investigation, the Immigration and Naturalization Service, and the Drug Enforcement Administration, as well as police chiefs from major cities. Following the summit, the IACP made a series of recommendations, including:

1. *Declaration of a National Commitment* to address violent crime, including the establishment of a Presidential Commission on Crime and Violence.
2. *Restrictions on firearms* purchases, limiting sale and manufacture of automatic and semiautomatic assault weapons.
3. *Fighting drugs* through educational programs, interdiction and detection programs, and incarceration of violent and non-violent offenders.
4. *Combating the influence of gangs* by gathering intelligence, enacting new laws directed at illegal gang activity, enacting juvenile justice reforms, and encouraging multijurisdictional cooperation.[37]

Many of the nation's largest law enforcement organizations supported the crime prevention measures in the recent federal crime bill. When these measures came under attack following the political shifts in the recent elections, the 250,000-member Fraternal Order of Police (FOP) issued a statement strongly opposing efforts to remove the new law's resources and crime prevention programs: "Crime problems require law enforcement *and* social remedies," said Richard Boyd, Director of Member Services for the National FOP.[38]

The death penalty actually hinders the fight against crime.

—Robert M. Morgenthau,
Manhattan District Attorney

One law enforcement group representing more than 35,000 individual members, the National Black Police Association, has a specific policy *against* the death penalty. Instead, they emphasize programs that control drugs, handgun control, and community policing to combat the problems of crime.[39]

Other law enforcement organizations, such as the Police Foundation and the Police Executive Research Forum, are focused primarily on research. They explore topics and produce publications on such topics as community policing, the effects of drugs on crime, and a host of issues of concern to those in law enforcement. Again, the death penalty is not one of their areas of concern.[40]

Police chiefs are not alone in their strong reservations about the effectiveness of the death penalty. Robert Morgenthau, Manhattan's District Attorney for the past twenty years, recently said that the failure of the death penalty is actually a well-kept secret among many prosecutors as well: "Prosecutors," he wrote in the *New York Times*, "must reveal the dirty little secret they too often share only among themselves: The death penalty actually hinders the fight against crime."[41]

Increasingly, crime prevention is a question of resources. "Executions," said Morgenthau, "waste scarce law-enforcement financial and personnel resources."[42]

Police chiefs and law enforcement organizations are deeply concerned about solutions to the crime problem facing this country. They come to this crisis with years of experience on the front line of doing whatever is in their power to reduce crime. They support those programs that will have a clear impact. Community policing, neighborhood crime programs, gun control, and a focused approach to certain kinds of crime, such as drug crime and youth crime, are among the approaches they recommend most strongly. They are equally clear that the problem of violence is not one which can be left to law enforcement to solve. Stronger families and neighborhoods, intervention on behalf of youth, and a sound economy with sufficient jobs are all necessary steps to a safer society.

Police chiefs are demonstrably less supportive of solutions like the death penalty, which merely sound tough but produce little return for the large amount of money invested. Some in law enforcement are totally opposed to capital punishment; others support it in theory. But few would give it the high priority accorded it in political campaigns and in legislative agendas designed mostly for sound bites and quick fixes.

Methodology of the Hart Poll

A total of 386 daytime telephone interviews were conducted with randomly designated police chiefs and county sheriffs throughout the U.S., excluding Alaska and Hawaii, between January 17 and 24, 1995. The margin of error is no more than ±6 percentage points with a 95% confidence level.

References

1. Remarks at the National Press Club, July 1, 1993.

2. Press release, Death Penalty Information Center, Oct. 27, 1992.

3. R. Morgenthau, "What Prosecutors Won't Tell You," *New York Times*, Feb. 7, 1995, at A25.

4. R. Abramson, "Emphasis on Values Is Needed to Stem Crime, Williams Says," *Los Angeles Times*, April 27, 1992, at B1, 4.

5. See P. Cook & D. Slawson, *The Costs of Processing Murder Cases in North Carolina* 97, 98 (May, 1993).

6. J. Mattox, "Texas' Death Penalty Dilemma," *Dallas Morning News*, Aug. 25, 1993.

7. *Violent Crime Control and Law Enforcement Act of 1994: Briefing Book*, U.S. Dept. of Justice, Sept. 24, 1994.

8. C. Krauss, "A Safer, If Not Safe, City: Crime Falls in New York," *New York Times*, Jan. 1, 1995, at 1.

9. See T. Squitieri, "Murder Rate Is Up in Usually Slow First Quarter," *USA Today,* April 3, 1992, at 8A.

10. "'Staggering' Crime Rate Drops: Cities Point to Police Strategies Behind the Decrease," *Law Enforcement News,* Jan.15, 1994, at 1.

11. Ibid.

12. E. Meyer, "Policing with People in Mind," *Washington Post,* June 15, 1992, at A1, 8.

13. G. James, "Having to Sell an Old Idea: the Cop on the Beat," *New York Times,* Oct. 9, 1991, at B1.

14. "'Attaboy' for Community Policing: Two-State Survey Finds Strong Faith in New Approach," *Law Enforcement News,* Sept. 15, 1994, at 1.

15. T. Rohrlich, "Does Death Penalty Deter Killers? No Clear Answer," *Los Angeles Times,* Mar. 23, 1990, at A1, 26.

16. R. Dugger, "In the Dead of the Night," *Texas Observer,* April 22, 1988, at 7.

17. Testimony of Gregory Ruff before the Kansas Senate, Committee on State and Federal Affairs, Feb. 18, 1994, on file with the Death Penalty Information Center.

18. See note 4.

19. *Crime in the United States, 1993,* U.S. Dept. of Justice, at p. 283 (Dec. 1994).

20. N. Gibbs, "Laying Down the Law," *Time,* Aug. 23, 1993, at 23, 25.

21. C. Krauss, "No Crystal Ball Needed on Crime," *New York Times,* Nov. 13, 1994 (projecting large increases in the 15-to-19-year-old population in the next 10 years).

22. See note 20.

23. "Line-of-Duty Deaths Continue Their Upward Trend in the '90s," *Law Enforcement News,* Jan. 15, 1994.

24. W. Bailey & R. Peterson, "Murder, Capital Punishment, and Deterrence: A Review of the Evidence and an Examination of Police Killings," 50 *Journal of Social Issues* 53, 71 (1994).

25. *Violent Crime in America: Recommendations of the IACP Summit on Violent Crime,* International Association of Chiefs of Police, April 27, 1993, at p.5.

26. Ibid.

27. See, e.g., statements by the National Association of Police Organizations (NAPO) in support of the gun control measures in the Violent Crime Control and Law Enforcement Act of 1994. Robert Scully, executive director of NAPO, speaking in praise of the Act, said: "[T]he American public wanted something done with guns. Despite all of the time, effort and money that was spent by the NRA, the American public was wise enough to see through it and still demanded that something be done about guns." *Law Enforcement News,* Dec. 31, 1994, at 1, 15. For a list of other police organizations supporting this law, see *ibid* at 14.

28. "Executions: The Brutal Facts," *New York Daily News,* Oct. 12, 1994.

29. "Criminal Use of Guns Increasing, Government Says," *Dallas Morning News,* Feb. 27, 1994, at 5A.

30. B. Herbert, "Deadly Data on Handguns," *New York Times,* Mar. 2, 1994.

31. See J. Socolovsky, "European Countries Attribute Low Murder Rate to Gun Laws," *Gainesville (Fla.) Sun,* May 19, 1991, at 1G.

32. F. Butterfield, "Cities Finding a New Policy Limits Guns," *New York Times,* Nov. 20, 1994, at 22.

33. *Profile of Inmates in the United States and in England and Wales, 1991,* U.S. Dept. of Justice, at p. 2 (Oct. 1994).

34. See note 2 (quoting Ronald Hampton).

35. See, e.g., *Sentencing for Life: Americans Embrace Alternatives to the Death Penalty,* Death Penalty Information Center (1993) (national poll shows more Americans support life without parole plus restitution than the death penalty).

36. *A National Action Plan to Combat Violent Crime: Recommendations of Mayors and Police Chiefs to the President of the United States,* The U.S. Conference of Mayors, Dec. 9, 1993, at p. 1–6.

37. See note 25 (Executive Overview).

38. *Police 'Oppose' Sniping at the Crime Bill,* electronic press release, Fraternal Order of Police, Sept. 27, 1994 (emphasis added).

39. Statements and resolutions of the National Black Police Association, Washington, DC, on file with the Death Penalty Information Center.

40. See recent publication lists of the Police Foundation and the Police Executive Research Forum, Washington, DC, on file with the Death Penalty Information Center (no mention of capital punishment in publication topics).

41. See note 3.

42. Ibid.

5

Criminals Are Not Deterred by the Death Penalty

Michael Ross

Michael Ross, #127404, is an inmate at the correctional institute in Somers, Connecticut. He was convicted in 1987 of capital felony murder in the deaths of five teenage girls and a twenty-three-year-old woman and was given six death sentences and two life sentences. After appeals, the state Supreme Court in 1994 upheld the convictions but overturned the death sentences because the judge had acted improperly by excluding evidence regarding Ross's mental condition. Since then, Ross has said he wants to avoid going through another penalty phase and to spare the victims' families another trial. He has told prosecutors he is willing to "go into the courtroom and admit to my actions, to accept responsibility for my actions and to accept the death penalty as punishment for those actions." He still believes the death penalty is wrong.

When the Supreme Court lifted the moratorium on capital punishment in 1976, it listed two social purposes: deterrence and retribution. But studies in the United States have shown that capital punishment has no deterrent effect, and the vast majority of developed democratic countries have abolished the death penalty because it is ineffective and inhumane. Capital punishment fails as a deterrent because murderers who premeditate about a killing do not expect to get caught, and spontaneous, emotional murderers are incapable of thinking rationally about the consequences of their act. Retribution also fails as reason to execute criminals because capital punishment violates a society's self-respect and humanity, and it is not always possible in a court of law to fairly and unemotionally make the decision to execute someone. Alternatives to the death penalty should be guided by the values of an enlightened and humanistic society, including compassion, mercy, and respect for human rights. Life sentences are adequate to ensure the public's safety and appeal to humanity's higher nature.

Reprinted, by permission of the publisher, from Michael Ross, "A View from Death Row," *Human Rights*, Summer 1995. Copyright © 1995, American Bar Association.

"**Y**ou shall have the punishment of death inflicted on you by electrocution."

With those words, I joined the almost 3,000 men and women currently on death row in America.

Since that chilling sentence was given to me in 1987, I've had plenty of time to think about the issue of capital punishment. I am well educated (a Cornell University graduate), but I never took the time to think about the death penalty in any great detail before—and my degree certainly never prepared me for death row.

When the U.S. Supreme Court lifted its moratorium on capital punishment in 1976, it ruled that "in any given case . . ." the death penalty must "measurably contribute" to one or both of two "social purposes—deterrence and retribution. . . ."

Let's examine these two criteria, but keep in mind that a constitutional justification for a punishment doesn't automatically make it morally right. After all, in the past the Court has found constitutional justification for, among other things, slavery, the prevention of women's voting rights, and other forms of sexual and racially discriminatory practices.

The most common justification given for capital punishment is that it is a supposedly superior deterrent to murder than to simply lock someone up for life.

But anyone who seriously offers this rationale is making a gut-level, emotional response without stopping to examine the issues.

Numerous studies over the past 30 years have attempted to find a connection between the use of the death penalty and homicide rates. Researchers have repeatedly found that capital punishment has no discernible effect on murder rates. In the United States, every study has shown that there is no significant difference between the murder rates of those states with active capital punishment laws and those of demographically similar, noncapital states.

International opposition

Outside of the United States, the vast majority of developed democratic countries have already abolished the death penalty. And almost to a country, each can boast of murder rates significantly lower than our own.

For example, Canada abolished the death penalty for murder in 1976. Ten years later, then–Prime Minister Brian Mulroney made a speech to the House of Commons in which he pointed out that in the 10 years following the abolition of the death penalty, the homicide rate in Canada had reached a 15-year low.

Internationally, the United Nations concluded, in a report for the Congress on the Prevention of Crime and the Treatment of Offenders, that "[d]espite much more advanced research efforts mounted to determine the deterrent value of the death penalty, no conclusive evidence has been obtained on its efficacy. . . ."

This, among other considerations, led the United Nations General Assembly to affirm that member states, "in order to guarantee fully the right to life, provided for in Article 3 of the Universal Declaration of Human Rights," should seek to progressively restrict "the number of offenses for which capital punishment may be imposed, with a view to the desirability of abolishing this punishment in all countries."

Many distinguished and well-known individuals have also taken a public stand against the death penalty. For example, the French statesman Marquis de Lafayette stated: "I shall ask for the abolition of the death penalty until I have the infallibility of human judgment demonstrated to me."

Andrei Sakharov, the Soviet human rights crusader, wrote, "I regard the death penalty as a savage and immoral institution which undermines the moral and legal foundations of a society. . . . I reject the notion that the death penalty has any essential deterrent effect on potential offenders. I am convinced that the contrary is true—that savagery begets only savagery."

And in America, U.S. Supreme Court Justice Harry Blackmun stated, "I feel morally and intellectually obligated simply to concede that the death penalty experiment has failed."

The deterrence hypothesis

Still, regardless of what the studies show and what knowledgeable people say, many will continue to insist that a system of "kill and be killed" is a deterrent.

What they are assuming is that a murderer thinks as rationally as they do. Clearly, this is a mistaken assumption. As former U.S. Supreme Court Justice Thurgood Marshall wrote, "The error in the hypothesis lies in the assumption that because people fear death more than life imprisonment after they are convicted, they necessarily must weigh potential penalties prior to committing criminal acts. . . . It is extremely unlikely that much thought is given to penalties before the act is committed."

It is the premeditated crime that society deems the most reprehensible, yet this type of crime is the least likely to be deterred by the threat of capital punishment. This is simply because in a premeditated crime the person doesn't expect to be caught.

I have been incarcerated for more than 10 years now and I have yet to meet anyone who expected to be caught and punished for their crimes. Rather, they expect to get away with it because of good planning. There can be no deterrent value in a punishment that one does not ever expect to receive.

A second type of murder is equally unlikely to be deterred by capital punishment: the spontaneous, emotionally driven murder. Such a murderer doesn't think about the possibility of getting caught, or cooly consider the foreseeable consequences of their actions. Emotions cloud the thought process. The person is not acting on something, but reacting to something. Emotions effectively diminish the capacity for reason. Fear of death, in itself, will not prevent this type of crime.

To continue to argue that deterrence is a reason to continue doling out the death penalty is to simply ignore the facts. But this will probably continue because, as social psychiatrist Dane Archer, a world-renowned authority on homicide, explains: "Revenge is a powerful undercurrent in all societies, including our own. I believe that the deterrence hypothesis is frequently nothing more than a veneer for revenge."

Let's move on to the Court's second justification for capital punishment—retribution. As renowned author Thorsten Sellen once wrote: "The struggle about this punishment has been one between ancient and deeply rooted beliefs in retribution, atonement or vengeance on the one hand, and, on the other, beliefs in the personal value and dignity of the common man. . . .

There can be no deterrent value in a punishment that one does not ever expect to receive.

Retribution has at its core the logic of the crude proportionality of "an eye for an eye." Indeed, it is often stated that the death penalty is a "just punishment in kind" for murder. But we have to be careful to make the necessary distinction between society's need for "justice" and the crime victim's desire for personal retribution.

As Justice Marshall often pointed out: "The purely retributive justification for the death penalty—that the death penalty is appropriate, not because of the beneficial effect on society, but because the taking of a murderer's [life] is itself morally good" is in itself morally repugnant.

We don't burn the arsonist's home, rape the rapist, nor steal from the thief. Obviously, the form of the punishment must adhere to and be limited by the standards of decency that govern society.

In the words of Lord Chancellor Gardiner, spoken during the 1965 death penalty abolition debates in the British Parliament: "When we abolished the punishment for treason that you should be hanged and then cut down while still alive, then disemboweled while still alive, and then quartered, we did not abolish that punishment because we sympathized with traitors, but because we took the view that this was a punishment no longer consistent with our self-respect."

It's not sympathy towards the murderer that is felt; indeed, most of us feel a great deal of anger and revulsion towards all murderers and their actions. The objection is that it is a complete renunciation of all that is embodied in our concept of humanity.

While the concept of retribution is a valid one, as the courts have found, it is "clear that channeling retributive instincts requires the state to do more than simply replicate the punishment that private vengeance would exact. To do less is simply to socialize vigilantism." While "punishment in kind" may sound good to the average citizen, it is seldom true "justice."

A major problem with retribution is that it is a difficult concept to deal with in a solely factual context. The judicial system is supposedly fair and just, evenhanded, appropriately administered, not arbitrary, capricious or random. But retribution, by its very nature, is an emotional issue, especially when dealing with some of the more serious or heinous crimes.

Capital cases in general tend to be sensationalized and emotionally charged affairs, and quite often it becomes almost impossible for a jury to dig through all those emotions to reach the underlying facts that they need to make a fair and just decision of life or death.

The High Court has ruled that "it is of vital importance to the defendant and to the community that any decision to impose the death penalty be—and appear to be—based on reason rather than caprice or emotion." Unfortunately the Court neglected to explain how this could be accomplished.

So how do we make the distinction between retribution and mindless emotionalism? In the context of capital punishment, one is supposed justice, yet the other is nothing more than the purposeless and needless imposition of pain and suffering.

Perhaps former U.S. Supreme Court Justice William Brennan was correct when he observed that "given the emotions generated by capital trials, it may be that juries, trial judges, and appellate courts considering sentences of death are invariably affected by impermissible considerations."

Maybe it is time for us to admit that we are not always capable of fairly making such a decision. And if we are, do we really wish to execute our criminals merely to get "even" with them?

Our politicians often leap at the chance to sound tough on crime. They are playing on the strong feelings of anxiety, frustration and anger that most people feel toward the seemingly uncontrollable plague of crime that our country is experiencing.

Such rhetoric detracts from the real work at hand of developing genuine programs for crime prevention and control. As such, the death penalty becomes the perfect political red herring—a program that sounds tough and effective and helps to create a false sense of security.

In reality, it saps our already limited resources.

Alternatives to capital punishment

There are acceptable alternatives to capital punishment that are more in line with the values of our supposedly enlightened and humanistic society. The state is supposed to be the pillar of our ideals, and its institutions should emulate the best values of our society.

Are not the greatest of these values our compassion, our concern for human rights, and our capacity for mercy? By continuing to conduct executions under either the pretense of deterrence or retribution, aren't we undermining the very foundations of our greatness? As Zimbabwe poet Chenjerai Hove wrote, "The death sentence is abominable, as abominable as the crime itself. Our state must be based on love, not hatred and victimization. Our penal code must be based on rehabilitation rather than annihilation."

No legal order can sustain itself unless it reflects an underlying moral order of society.

There are suitable alternatives. Individuals who are a danger to society must be removed from society. Society has the right to protect itself; there is no question about that. If rehabilitation is not possible or is not a consideration, then that removal must be made permanent. Society demands protection and has a right to protect its citizens.

Those who favor the abolition of the death penalty do not advocate releasing convicted murderers into society. The choice is not between the death penalty and unconditional release, but between the death penalty and a meaningful life sentence. Life without the possibility of parole, or natural life sentences, meets the necessary requirements of society.

By replacing capital punishment with a guarantee that the offender will not be released back into society at some future date, you eliminate the perceived need for the death penalty and greatly diminish society's desire for it. The public is not interested so much in the death penalty as it is in a guarantee that individuals who commit murder will not be released back into society to commit new crimes.

A national poll taken in 1993 confirms this point. Seventy-seven percent of those interviewed said that the death penalty is appropriate for those convicted of killing in cold blood.

Only 41 percent favored it if the alternative was life without the possibility of parole with restitution being made to the victim's family.

The public is not interested so much in the death penalty as it is in a guarantee that individuals who commit murder will not be released back into society to commit new crimes.

As the Supreme Court once ruled: "The state thereby suffers nothing and loses no power. The purpose of punishment is fulfilled; crime is repressed by penalties of just, not tormenting, severity; its repetition is prevented, and hope is given for the reformation of the criminal."

Abolition is humane

Retribution, vengeance, blood atonement and the like are difficult feelings to suppress. Perhaps I, and individuals like myself, "deserve" to die. But in light of suitable alternatives, such as natural life sentences, is society paying too high a price when it executes its own citizens?

Justice Marshall once wrote: "I cannot agree that the American people have been so hardened, so embittered that they want to take the life of one who performs even the basest criminal act knowing that the execution is nothing more than bloodlust."

It is time for us to acknowledge the death penalty for what it really is rather than for what we wish it to be. By rejecting the simple solutions that compromise our values and undermine the fundamental principles of our society, we maintain the greatness of our country.

By giving in to our basest emotions we lower ourselves to the level of the very persons that we wish to execute, and in the process weaken the moral fibers that bind and protect our society.

When we recognize the humanity of even the vilest criminals, when we acknowledge them as fellow human beings rather than as objects to be discarded, we pay ourselves the highest of tributes and celebrate our own humanity.

6

Criminals Are Deterred by the Death Penalty

Joseph Sobran

Joseph Sobran is a conservative syndicated columnist.

A news item proves that the death penalty is a deterrent: A witness to a murder decides not to testify and chooses instead to go to jail for contempt of court because an earlier witness had been murdered for testifying. This story confirms that people are deterred from committing acts that could result in death. Criminals know that the threat of death motivates people and enables them to commit crimes. The fear of death is a fundamental human motive, and criminals, in this respect, are no different from other people.

Is the death penalty a deterrent?

This old and hotly disputed question has now been answered: Yes. The answer arrived on, of all things, the front page of the liberal *Washington Post*.

I didn't expect the liberal *Post* to confirm such a reactionary position. And maybe it didn't mean to. But the only conclusion you can draw from the front-page story is that the death penalty works.

Ask the criminals

The headline is "D.C. Witness Imprisoned by Fear." Subhead: "Man Goes to Jail Rather than Risk Testifying at Murder Trial." An earlier witness to a murder had been slain hours after testifying, so a second witness to the same murder, Arlin Budoo, decided he'd rather face the certainty of imprisonment for contempt of court than the strong possibility of death.

But of course! How simple! Why didn't anyone think of this before? All these years we've been trying to answer the deterrence question by asking criminologists for their opinions. How awfully pedantic!

Why didn't we just ask the criminals?

The criminal community is largely dedicated to the proposition that if you plausibly threaten to kill people, they will do what you want them to do. The mere awareness of violent criminals is enough to deter most of us from wandering in our big cities at night.

The criminal community is largely dedicated to the proposition that if you plausibly threaten to kill people, they will do what you want them to do.

The point is that criminals, their minds unclouded by the latest criminological thinking, assume that people are deterred by a death penalty, even if it be privately administered. "Privately" may be the operative word. The private execution is uncomplicated by red tape, legal ritual, the law's delays, the pangs of despised love, etc. It is performed under something like laboratory conditions.

The fear of death

Thomas Hobbes built his whole political philosophy on the premise that the fear of death is one of the most basic human motives. He didn't think this was an arcane theory; he thought it was so obvious that it was a sound starting point for all further theorizing.

Our criminal class agrees with Hobbes; our ruling class doesn't. Which probably explains a lot about the state of American society today. Even if the death penalty doesn't deter any more effectively than a stiff prison sentence, its active existence sends out the message that the community is resolved to defend itself. Today all the resolution is on the criminal side.

You can still argue that the death penalty degrades the society that uses it, the way torture does. Even if some criminals deserve the rack and its use would deter others, we are not about to adopt it. And if that means more Polly Klaas cases, too bad. [Twelve-year-old Polly Klaas was kidnapped and murdered by Richard Allen Davis in 1993. Davis, who had spent most of his life behind bars and had been paroled only three months before the kidnapping, was sentenced to death in 1996.]

Everything deters somebody. Nothing deters everybody. Even the likelihood of being caught and tortured to death would not eliminate crime. On the other hand, even the remote chance of being arrested and tried causes many people to observe the law. Adding a death penalty wouldn't significantly lower the crime rate among white liberals.

The death penalty shouldn't be thought of as a "policy option." If it's justified, we have a moral obligation to kill men like Polly Klaas' killer. If it's not justified, then even its deterrent effect can't justify it.

But let's not be silly. Death deters. Obviously.

7

The Death Penalty May Increase Homicide Rates

Michael J. Godfrey and Vincent Schiraldi

Vincent Schiraldi is the founder and Executive Director of the Center on Juvenile and Criminal Justice (CJCJ) in San Francisco. Schiraldi has served on government commissions dealing with prison overcrowding, juvenile probation, and minorities and crime, and has published numerous commentaries on juvenile and criminal justice issues. Michael J. Godfrey is a research assistant at CJCJ.

The most frequently used argument to justify death sentences is that executing a person convicted of a capital crime deters other people from committing the same crime. Studies, though, have failed to show that homicide rates fall immediately after executions; to the contrary, an increase in homicides is not uncommon after a publicized execution. This phenomenon, known as a "brutalization effect," was demonstrated in California, where the homicide rate increased in the months immediately following executions in 1992 and 1993. Similarly, the murder rate in California grew faster during execution years than in nonexecution years. Because capital punishment has not been proven to deter crime, and may in fact "lead by example," the death penalty has failed.

"It is the deed that teaches, not the name we give it. Murder and capital punishment are not opposites that cancel one another, but similars that breed their kind."
—George Bernard Shaw

". . . we are the only Western democracy that still has capital punishment. In my view it should be abolished. Let me add just this: It does not deter murders. It serves no purpose."
—Retired U.S. Supreme Court Justice Lewis R. Powell, Jr.

In more than three centuries since Daniel Frank became the first person to be lawfully executed in the New World for the crime of theft, there have been an estimated 18,000 to 20,000 persons put to death.[1] In California, the numbers of those executed are staggering. Since 1893, there

Reprinted from Michael J. Godfrey and Vincent Schiraldi, "How Have Homicide Rates Been Affected by California's Death Penalty?" *In Brief,* a publication of the Center on Juvenile and Criminal Justice, April 1995, by permission.

have been a total of 504 executions in the state of California. In total executions since 1930, California is ranked fourth behind Georgia (383), Texas (368) and New York (329) at 294.[2]

April 21, 1995, marked the three year anniversary of Robert Alton Harris' execution. This was the first execution in California since Aaron Mitchell was put to death by lethal gas in 1967. At the age of 39, Harris ushered back California's era of capital punishment.

Since 1977, when capital punishment was reinstated, California has sentenced 363 prisoners to die on death row, and in addition to Harris, has executed one other, David Mason.[3] With the reinstitution of capital punishment in California, one of the arguments most frequently used to justify the death penalty is deterrence: that it is necessary to kill an offender to dissuade other people from committing the same kind of crime.

The deterrence argument

The "common sense" logic of this argument rests on questionable assumptions. If the death penalty did deter potential offenders more effectively than other punishments, then jurisdictions with the death penalty would have a lower rate of crime than those without. Similarly, a rise in the rate of crimes punishable by death would be expected in jurisdictions which abolish executions and a decline in crime rates would be expected among those which introduce it. Finally, one would expect a drop in homicide rates immediately following executions, particularly highly publicized ones. Yet, study after study has failed to establish any such link between the death penalty and homicide rates.

Conversely, an increase in homicides is not uncommon after a publicized execution and is generally referred to by scholars as a "brutalization effect."[4] Some research has suggested that executions may temporarily result in more homicides. William J. Bowers and Glenn L. Pierce analyzed monthly homicide rates from 1907 to 1963 in New York State (which carried out more executions than any other state during this period). They found that there had been, on average, two additional homicides in the month after an execution. They suggested that this momentary rise in homicides might be due to a "brutalizing" effect of executions, similar to the effect of other violent events such as publicized suicides, mass murders and assassinations. Similar findings have been made by other studies.[5]

One of the landmark studies with respect to deterrence and the death penalty was conducted by Thorsten Sellin in 1959.[6] A nationally renowned sociologist at the University of Pennsylvania, Sellin discovered through a comparison of abolitionist and retentionist states, that homicide rates in abolitionist states were not significantly different than the rates in retentionist states.[7] From this evidence he drew the "inevitable conclusion . . . that executions have no discernible effect on homicide death rates." These conclusions were a basic theme in the argument presented to the United States Supreme Court in 1971 to support a finding by the Court that the death penalty was a "cruel and unusual punishment."[8]

In a comparison of retentionist and abolitionist countries, homicide rates have been found to be greater in countries that use the death penalty than those which do not. In an analysis of selected countries, the five abolitionist countries with the highest homicide rate averaged a rate of 11.6 per 100,000 persons. The five retentionist countries with the highest homicide rate averaged a rate of 41.6 per 100,000 persons.[9] In other words, countries that have capital punishment appear to have higher murder rates than those countries that do not have capital punishment.

The United Kingdom Royal Commission on Capital Punishment (1949–1953) examined the available statistics on jurisdictions which had abolished or ceased using the death penalty for murder. From its survey of seven European countries, New Zealand, and individual states within Australia and the United States, the Commission concluded that "there is no clear evidence in any of the figures we have examined that the abolition of capital punishment has led to an increase in the homicide rate, or that its reintroduction has led to a fall."[10]

Executions and California's homicide rate

In this study, homicide rates were analyzed in 1992 and 1993 on a month-by-month basis.[11] Rates for the four month period preceding and following the executions of both Robert Alton Harris and David Mason were examined to discern evidence of a deterrent effect.

Additionally, the annual increase in the murder rates was compared during a period of fifteen years in which California carried out the death penalty, and the twenty-four years in which it did not.

In the four months of 1992 preceding Harris' highly publicized execution, the average number of monthly homicides was 306. In the four months following the execution, the average number of homicides per month was 333. This suggests the presence of a "brutalization effect" noted in previous studies.

In 1993, the year of David Mason's execution, homicides jumped from 12.5 per 100,000 persons in 1992 to 12.9 per 100,000 in 1993. In the four month period preceding Mason's death, there was an average of 362 homicides per month, compared to an average of 348 in the four months following his death (see Figure I).

A similar pattern is revealed when comparing the murder rates in California during its abolitionist and retentionist years. In a simple comparison during the retentionist period from 1952 to 1967, when executions occurred on average about every two months, homicide rates increased from 2.4 per 100,000 in 1952 to 6.0 per 100,000 in 1967.[12] Within this fifteen-year period, the homicide rate increased by 150%—an annual increase of 10%. Conversely, between the abolitionist period of 1967 and 1991, when no executions took place, the homicide rate increased from 6.0 per 100,000 to 12.6 per 100,000. Over this twenty-four year span, the homicide rate increased by 110% or 4.8% annually. In other words, the average annual increase in homicides was twice as high during years in which the death penalty was being carried out than in years during which no one was executed (see Figure II).[13]

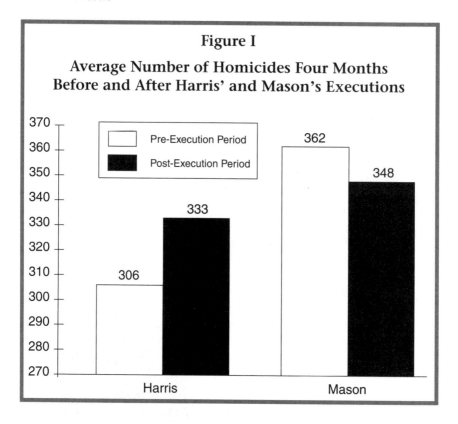

Figure I

Average Number of Homicides Four Months Before and After Harris' and Mason's Executions

Numerous previous studies indicate that there is no clear evidence that the death penalty deters. This study has shown that homicide rates are at best unaffected by capital punishment in California. An increase in homicides during times of both abolition and retention was found, with the retentionist increase more than double the abolitionist increase. This is consistent with the general increase in homicide rates that occurred after Harris' execution. In fact, immediately following Harris' execution, a "brutalizing effect" was evidenced which may be in response to the violent nature of executions and the extraordinary publicity which Harris' execution received.

In sum, the evidence suggests that there is no reduction in homicides due to the death penalty, and that the death penalty may, in fact, "lead by example." For proponents of the issue, this is unfortunate news. The deterrence argument is, for many, the primary argument for the use of the death penalty. In review of this study, it is apparent that no such deterrent effect exists.

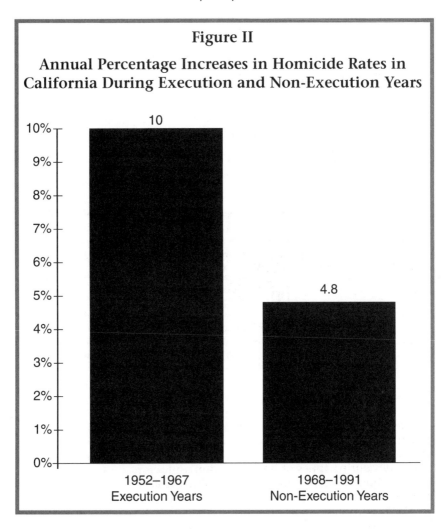

Figure II

Annual Percentage Increases in Homicide Rates in California During Execution and Non-Execution Years

Notes:

1. Bedau, H.A., editor, *The Death Penalty in America,* Oxford University Press, New York, 1982, p. 3.

2. Bureau of Justice Statistics Bulletin, *Capital Punishment in America,* 1993, p. 11.

3. Ibid., p. 1.

4. This "brutalization effect" is argued to be the consequence of the "beastly example" that an execution presents (Beccaria, Cesare [1963], *On Crimes and Punishments,* translated by H. Paolucci [1764]. Indianapolis: Bobbs-Merrill). Ostensibly, executions devalue human life and "demonstrate that it is correct and appropriate to kill those who have gravely offended us," (Bowers, William J. and Glenn Pierce [1980], "Deterrence or Brutalization:

What Is the Effect of Executions?" *Crime and Delinquency* 26: 453-484).
The lesson taught by execution may be the legitimacy of lethal vengeance
not deterrence.

5. A monthly time-series analysis of executions and first-degree murders in
    Chicago, Illinois, from 1915 to 1921, produced findings consistent with
    those of Bowers and Pierce: William C. Bailey, "Disaggregation in Deter-
    rence and Death Penalty Research: The Case of Murder in Chicago," *Jour-
    nal of Criminal Law and Criminology,* vol. 74, no. 3, 1983, pp. 827-859.

6. Sellin, T., "The Death Penalty: A Report for the Model Penal Code Project
    of the American Law Institute," *Capital Punishment,* 25 Fed. Probation 3;
    September 1961.

7. "Retentionist" generally refers to states and territories which retain and
    use the death penalty for ordinary crimes. "Abolitionist" refers to states
    and territories whose laws do not provide for the death penalty for any
    crime.

8. Baldus, D.C. & Cole, W.L., "A Comparison of the Work of Thorsten Sellin
    and Isaac Ehrlich on the Deterrent Effect of Capital Punishment," *Yale
    Law Journal,* vol. 85: 170, 1985.

9. Amnesty International, "When the State Kills," *The Death Penalty: A Hu-
    man Rights Issue,* Amnesty International Publications, 1989; homicide
    data was taken from the International Criminal Police Organization (In-
    terpol), International Crime Statistics, 1989–90. To uphold consistency,
    the U.S. crime rates were also taken from Interpol. GENERAL POPULA-
    TION DATA: most figures are from the 1994 World Almanac, which lists
    population data from 1992; some general population figures came from
    Interpol.

10. United Kingdom Royal Commission on Capital Punishment 1949–1953.
    A report presented to Parliament by command of Her Majesty. Her
    Majesty's Stationary Office. London, 1953, pp. 23, 358–359.

11. All of the crime figures in this section are from: California Department of
    Justice, Law Enforcement Information Center, Willful Homicide Crimes,
    1990–1993. This is a monthly account of the total number of reported
    homicides during these years. Homicide rate information is obtained
    from the annual report entitled Department of Justice, Division of Law
    Enforcement Information Center, *Crime and Delinquency in California,*
    1993, p. 108.

12. Bowers, W.J., Pierce, G.L., McDevitt, J.F., *Legal Homicide: Death as Punish-
    ment in America,* Northeastern University Press, 1984.

13. Department of Justice, Division of Law Enforcement Information Center,
    Crime and Delinquency in California, 1993, p. 108.

8

The Death Penalty May Save Innocent Lives

Ernest van den Haag

Ernest van den Haag is the retired John M. Olin Professor of Jurisprudence and Public Policy at Fordham University in New York City.

A study of the effects of executions on the murder rate has concluded that every execution of a murderer deters, on average, eighteen murders that would have occurred without it. The same study has also concluded that a small (1 percent) increase in murder convictions would deter 105 murders. Researchers have not yet proven conclusively that capital punishment either is or is not a more effective deterrent than life imprisonment. But even if an execution has only a small chance of deterring future murders, the murderer should be executed because he has, through his crime, forfeited his life. Capital punishment satisfies justice, and the fact that it may also save lives is enough to favor the execution of convicted murderers.

Professor Stephen K. Layson, an economist at the University of North Carolina at Greensboro, has published in the *Southern Economic Journal* (July 1985) a statistical study of the effects of executions on the murder rate. He concluded that every execution of a murderer deters, on the average, 18 murders that would have occurred without it.

Layson also inquired into the effects of the arrest and conviction of murderers on the murder rate. His correlations indicate that a 1 per cent increase in the clearance (arrest) rate for murder would lead to 250 fewer murders per year. Currently the clearance rate is 75 per cent. Further, a 1 per cent increase in murder convictions would deter about 105 murders. Currently 38 per cent of all murders result in a conviction; 0.1 per cent of murders result in an execution.

Correlating murder and punishment rates

Attempts to correlate murder to punishment rates have been made for a long time. Most had flagrant defects. Some correlated murder rates to the

Reprinted, by permission, from Ernest van den Haag, "Death and Deterrence," *National Review*, March 14, 1986; © 1986 by National Review, Inc., 215 Lexington Ave., New York, NY 10016.

presence or absence of capital-punishment statutes—not to executions, which alone matter. Others failed properly to isolate murder rates from variables other than punishment, even when these variables were known to influence murder rates. For instance, changes in the proportion of young males in the population do influence murder rates regardless of executions, since most murders are committed by young males. The first major statistical analysis that properly handled all variables was published by Isaac Ehrlich in the *American Economic Review* (June 1975). Ehrlich found that from 1933 to 1969 "an additional execution per year . . . may have resulted on the average in seven or eight fewer murders."

Ehrlich's study went against the cherished beliefs of most social scientists (after all, it confirmed what common sense tells us). A whole cottage industry arose to refute him. In turn he refuted the refuters. The verdict is inconclusive. As is often the case in statistical matters, if a different period is analyzed, or some technical assumptions are changed, a different result is produced. Thus the testimony of Professor Thorsten Sellin, given in 1953—long before Ehrlich wrote—to the Royal Commission on Capital Punishment in Great Britain, still stands. Asked whether he could "conclude . . . that capital punishment has no deterrent effect," Sellin, an ardent but honest opponent of capital punishment, replied, "No, there is no such conclusion." Despite considerable advances in methods of analysis I think that, as yet, it has not been proved conclusively that capital punishment deters more than life imprisonment, or that it does not. However, the preponderance of evidence now does tend to show that capital punishment deters more than alternative punishments. Professor Layson's paper will add to that preponderance. But many attempts will be made to refute it, and, in all likelihood, the verdict will still be that the statistics are not conclusive.

What are we to deduce? Obviously people fear death more than life imprisonment. Only death is final. Where there is life there is hope. Actual murderers feel that way: 99.9 per cent prefer life imprisonment to death. So will prospective murderers. What is feared most deters most. Possibly, statistics do not show this clearly, because there are so few executions compared to the number of murders. It is even possible that the uncertain prospect of execution deters so few not already deterred by the prospect of life imprisonment that there is no statistical trace. Yet, if by executing convicted murderers there is any chance, even a mere possibility, of deterring future murderers, I think we should execute them. The life even of a few victims who may be spared seems infinitely precious to me. The life of the convicted murderer has but negative value. His crime has forfeited it.

Beyond deterrence

Opponents of capital punishment usually admit that their opposition has little to do with statistical data. When asked whether they would favor the death penalty if it were shown conclusively that each execution deters, say, one hundred murders, such opponents as Ramsey Clark (former U.S. attorney general) or Henry Schwarzschild (ACLU) resoundingly say no. But neither likes the inference that must be drawn: that he is more interested in keeping murderers alive than in sparing their victims, that he values the life of a convicted murderer more than the life of innocent victims. Those who do not share this bizarre valuation will favor capital punishment.

For beyond deterrence, or possible deterrence, there is justice. The thought that the man who cruelly and deliberately slaughtered your child for fun or profit is entitled peacefully to live out his days at taxpayers' expense, playing tennis or baseball or enjoying the prison library, is hard to stomach. Wherefore about 75 per cent of Americans favor the death penalty, for the sake of justice, and to save innocent lives. I think they are right.

If by executing convicted murderers there is any chance, even a mere possibility, of deterring future murderers, I think we should execute them.

On occasion I have been presented with a hypothetical. Suppose, I have been asked, that each execution were shown to raise rather than reduce the murder rate. Of course this is quite unlikely (wherefore there is no serious evidence): The more severe and certain the punishment, the less often the crime occurs, all other things being equal. The higher the price of anything, the less is bought. But, if one accepts, *arguendo,* the hypothetical, the answer depends on whether one prefers justice—which demands the execution of the murderer—or saving the lives that, by this hypothesis, could be saved by not executing him. I love justice, but I love innocent lives more. I would prefer to save them.

Fortunately we do not face this dilemma. On the contrary. Capital punishment not only satisfies justice but is also more likely to save innocent lives than life imprisonment.

9

Most Experts Believe the Death Penalty Does Not Deter Crime

Michael L. Radelet and Ronald L. Akers

Michael L. Radelet is the chair of the department of sociology at the University of Florida. Ronald L. Akers is a professor of sociology at the University of Florida and the director of the school's Center for Studies in Criminology and Law.

Capital punishment has strong political and public support primarily because it is seen as a general deterrent. To find out what "experts" think of the deterrent value of the death penalty, a small and elite group of criminologists were polled on their views. Most experts, based on their knowledge of existing research, believe the death penalty has little or no impact on murder rates and is politically motivated. Many also believe the presence of a death penalty tends to increase a state's murder rate rather than decrease it. The authors hope that the informed views of criminologists will encourage politicians to rethink their advocacy of the death penalty.

The American public has long been favorably disposed toward capital punishment for convicted murderers, and that support continues to grow. In a 1981 Gallup Poll, two-thirds of Americans voiced general approval for the death penalty. That support rose to 72% in 1985, to 76% in 1991, and to 80% in 1994.[1] Although these polls need to be interpreted with extreme caution, it is clear that there are few issues on which more Americans agree: in at least some circumstances, death is seen as a justifiable punishment.

Part of the support for capital punishment comes from the belief that the death penalty is legitimate under a theory of "just desserts."[2] This justification suggests that murderers should be executed for retributive reasons: murderers should suffer, and the retributive effects of life imprisonment are insufficient for taking a life. While such views are worthy of debate,

Reprinted by special permission of Northwestern University School of Law from Michael L. Radelet and Ronald L. Akers, "Deterrence and the Death Penalty: The Views of the Experts," *Journal of Criminal Law and Criminology*, vol. 87, issue 1, pp. 1–16 (1996).

no empirical research can tell us if the argument is "correct" or "incorrect." Empirical studies can neither answer the question of what specific criminals (or non-criminals) "deserve," nor settle debates over other moral issues surrounding capital punishment.

Capital punishment as a deterrent

On the other hand, much of the support for capital punishment rests on its presumed value as a general deterrent: we need the death penalty to encourage potential murderers to avoid engaging in criminal homicide.[3] Politicians are often quick to use some version of the deterrence rationale in their cries for more and quicker executions when they see such appeals as a promising way to attract votes.[4]

Whether or not the threat or use of the death penalty is, has been, or could be a deterrent to homicide is an empirical question that should not—and cannot—be answered on the basis of moral or political stands. It is an empirical question that scores of researchers, dating back to a young Edwin Sutherland, writing in the pages of the *Journal of Criminal Law & Criminology*,[5] have examined.

Has this long history and sizeable body of research led to any general conclusions? Can any factual statement be made about the death penalty's deterrent effects, or are the scholarly studies such that no conclusions can be reached? At least two valid methods can be used to answer these questions. One is to examine individual scholarly opinions, as is done in most published research reports. Here researchers review the empirical research on deterrence and reach conclusions based on it and their own research. A second approach is to gauge the informed opinions of scholars or experts. Indeed, much research-based public policy rests on known or presumed consensus of "expert" opinions. It is the aim of this viewpoint to address the question of the death penalty's ability to deter homicides using this second approach: by gauging the judgments of a set of America's top criminologists.

Literature review

Measuring sentiment on the death penalty is not as easy a task as it might at first appear. When opinion polls ask respondents whether they support the death penalty, often no alternative punishments are given, and respondents are left to themselves to ponder what might happen if a particular inmate were not executed. Often respondents erroneously believe that absent execution, offenders will be released to the community after serving a short prison sentence.[6] Even the most ardent death penalty abolitionists might support capital punishment if the alternative was to have dangerous murderers quickly released from prison. When respondents are asked how they feel about the death penalty given an alternative of life without parole, support decreases significantly.[7] In 1991, Gallup found that 76% of Americans supported the death penalty, but that support would drop to 53% if life imprisonment without parole were available as an alternative.[8]

While most deterrence research has found that the death penalty has virtually the same effect as long-term imprisonment on homicide rates,[9] in the mid-1970's economist Isaac Ehrlich reported that he had uncovered a significant deterrent effect.[10] He estimated that each execution between 1933 and 1969 had prevented eight homicides.[11] This research gained widespread attention, in part because Solicitor General Robert Bork used it to defend the death penalty in the 1970s when the Supreme Court was considering whether to make permanent its 1972 ban of the death penalty.[12] Although scholars, including a panel appointed by the National Academy of Sciences,[13] strongly criticized Ehrlich's work for methodological and conceptual shortcomings,[14] some continue to cite it as proof that the death penalty does have a deterrent effect.[15] A student of Ehrlich's, Stephen Layson, later reported his estimate that each execution deterred approximately 18 homicides.[16] This research, too, was loudly criticized,[17] but nonetheless it continues to be embraced by proponents of the death penalty.[18]

The assumption of a deterrent effect is a major factor in public and political endorsement of the death penalty.

It could very well be that the mere *existence* of a critique is more important than the *quality* of that critique. One researcher finds one thing, and another claims to refute it. What is left is a net gain of zero: politicians who never read or understand the original studies can select either position and cite only those studies that support their position.

Some research has asked the general public whether the death penalty acts as a deterrent to murder. Such a question is regularly asked to national samples in Gallup Polls.[19] In the mid-1980's, just over 60% of the respondents in Gallup Polls said they believed the death penalty was a deterrent. Furthermore, these polls showed that the deterrence rationale is an important death penalty justification. In the 1986 Gallup Poll, respondents were asked if they would support the death penalty "if new evidence proved that the death penalty does not act as a deterrent to murder." Given this assumption of no deterrent effect, support for capital punishment dropped from 70% to 51%.[20]

Similarly, in the 1991 poll, where 76% of the respondents initially indicated support for the death penalty, Gallup asked those who favored the death penalty: "Suppose new evidence showed that the death penalty does *not* act as a deterrent to murder, that it does not lower the murder rate. Would you favor or oppose the death penalty?" As in the earlier poll, the respondents were less likely (76% vs. 52%) to support capital punishment if it were shown that it is not a deterrent to homicide.[21] These findings indicate that the assumption of a deterrent effect is a major factor in public and political endorsement of the death penalty. If that assumption is undermined, even those who initially favor the death penalty tend to move away from it.

In another study that sheds light on the public's view of the death penalty's deterrent abilities, Ellsworth and Ross mailed questionnaires to 500 northern California respondents.[22] Among their findings was that 82% of the death penalty proponents, but only 3.1% of the opponents, agreed with the statement, "We need capital punishment to show criminals that we really mean business about wiping out crime in this country."[23] The Gallup and Ellsworth/Ross surveys show that the assumption of deterrence is one of the most important foundations for death penalty support in America. Questions from both the Gallup and the Ellsworth/Ross surveys were used in our own research, so precise comparisons will be made when our results are discussed below.

One recent survey has been conducted that examines how leading police officials, who arguably hold more expertise on criminal behavior than the general public, view the deterrence rationale for capital punishment. The survey was conducted in 1995 by the Washington, D.C., based polling firm, Peter D. Hart Research Associates.[24] Telephone surveys were conducted with 386 randomly selected police chiefs and county sheriffs from throughout the U.S. Little support for the deterrence argument was found. Among six choices presented as "primary" ways to reduce violent crime, only 1% of the law enforcement respondents chose the death penalty. This choice ranked last among the options. When asked to consider the statement "The death penalty significantly reduces the number of homicides," 67% of the chiefs felt the statement was inaccurate, while only 26% said it was accurate. Reacting to the poll, former New York Police Chief Patrick V. Murphy wrote, "Like the emperor's new clothes, the flimsy notion that the death penalty is an effective law enforcement tool is being exposed as mere political puffery."[25] For comparative purposes, some of the questions we posed to our sample (reported below) were taken from this survey.

Methodology

In order to assess what the experts think about the deterrent effect of the death penalty, we must first define the term "expert." According to one definition, the law enforcement executives surveyed by Hart are experts. Another definition would include scholars who have conducted high-quality scholarly research on the death penalty and deterrence, such as the panel appointed two decades ago by the National Academy of Sciences.[26] A thorough literature review would document the views of these researchers, but such a survey would simply reflect disagreements that are evident in the scholarly literature, not evaluate or judge them.

But what about other leading criminologists who are not specialists in capital punishment research but who have gained more general visibility and leadership in the field? It is this group of "experts," as defined by visibility and recognition as leaders among professional criminologists, that we surveyed for this project. We operationally define "expert" as one who has been recognized by peers by being elected to the highest office in scholarly organizations. We contacted all present and former presidents of the country's top academic criminological societies. This small and elite group includes many of the country's most respected and distinguished criminologists. As such, although few of these scholars have done research on capital punishment or deterrence, they are generally well versed in central criminological issues, such as crime causation, crime prevention, and criminal justice policy issues. The presidents of three associations were surveyed: the American Society of Criminology, Academy of Criminal Justice Sciences, and the Law and Society Association.

The American Society of Criminology (ASC), founded in 1941, is the country's largest association of professional and academic criminologists, with a 1996 membership of 2,700.[27] The Academy of Criminal Justice Sciences (ACJS), founded in 1963, today includes 3,350 members.[28] Its membership overlaps to a considerable extent with the ASC, but its leadership (taken primarily from undergraduate teaching programs) does not. Only one person in the history of the two societies has served as president of both.[29] The Law and Society Association (LSA), founded in 1964, includes more law professors and legal scholars among its 1,400 members than either the ASC or ACJS.[30] Again there is overlapping membership with ASC and ACJS, but no one has served as president of LSA and either of the other two. These three associations are all interdisciplinary and publish what are among the most respected scholarly journals in criminology and criminal justice: *Criminology* (ASC), *Justice Quarterly* (ACJS), and *Law and Society Review* (LSA).

We began by obtaining names and addresses of current and all living former presidents of each of the three organizations. A total of seventy one individuals were identified: twenty nine from the Academy of Criminal Justice Sciences, twenty seven from the American Society of Criminology,[31] and fifteen from the Law and Society Association. As noted, one person had served as president of two of the associations, reducing our sample to seventy. Drafts of the questionnaire were critiqued by three scholars who have conducted deterrence research. Numbered questionnaires were mailed to our respondents, and follow-ups were sent to nonrespondents. In the end, a total of sixty seven responded (95.7%): twenty seven from ACJS, twenty six from the ASC, and fifteen from LSA.

The presidents were clearly asked in both the cover letter and on the questionnaire itself to answer the questions *on the basis of their knowledge of the literature and research in criminology*. We quite purposely did not ask for their personal opinions on the death penalty—information on this might be interesting, but it is irrelevant to the goal of the present study. Eleven questions, all relating to deterrence issues, were included on the questionnaire; the responses to all eleven are reported below.

General questions on deterrence

The first question explored concerns how the presidents generally view the deterrence question. Table 1 begins by replicating the question asked in the Gallup Polls, "Do you feel that the death penalty acts as a deterrent to the commitment of murder—that it lowers the murder rate, or what?" It can be seen that the criminologists are more than twice as likely as the general population to believe that the death penalty does *not* lower the murder rate—41% of the population held this belief in 1991, the last year that Gallup published responses to this question, compared to 83.6% of our experts. Among the sixty four presidents who voiced opinions on this question, fifty six (87.5%) believe the death penalty does not have deterrent effects.

Table 1 also compares responses to deterrence questions between our respondents and the members of the general public in northern California surveyed by Ellsworth and Ross. Here 86.5% of the criminologists and 46% of the general public say they are "sure" or "think" that "abolishing the death penalty (in a particular state) would not have any significant effects on the murder rate (in that state)." As would be expected, substantially more members of the general public than the criminologists (32.6% vs. 10.4%) say they have no idea whether this statement is true or false.

Similarly, as shown in the third part of Table 1, the criminologists are much less likely than members of the general public to agree that "Over the years, states which have had the death penalty have had lower murder rates than neighboring states which did not have a death penalty." Nearly 80% of the criminologists said that they were sure or they thought this was not true, compared to 37% of the general public. Interestingly, more criminologists stated that they had no idea whether this statement was true or false than did members of the general public (14.9% vs. 6.0%).

The results of Table 1 clearly show that approximately 80% of the experts in criminology believe, on the basis of the literature and research in criminology, that the death penalty does not have significant deterrent effects. In addition, no matter how measured, it is clear that the criminologists are much more likely than the general public to dismiss the deterrence argument.

Table 2 compares the beliefs of our experts to those of top criminal justice administrators, specifically to the beliefs of the police chiefs surveyed by Peter D. Hart Research Associates in 1995 (discussed above).[32] Overall there is widespread agreement between the criminologists and the police chiefs on the deterrent value of the death penalty (or lack thereof), with the criminologists even less likely than the chiefs to see any deterrent value. As seen in Table 2, all of the criminologists, and 85% of the police chiefs, believe it is totally or largely accurate that "politicians support the death penalty as a symbolic way to show they are tough on crime." Almost 87% of the criminologists and 57% of the chiefs find it totally or largely accurate to say that "debates about the death penalty distract Congress and state legislatures from focusing on real solutions to crime problems." None of the criminologists, and only about a quarter of the chiefs, believe there is any accuracy in the statement, "the death penalty significantly reduces the number of homicides." These statements indicate that both academic criminologists and police chiefs view the death penalty as more effective in political rhetoric than as a criminal justice tool.

Table 3 asks general questions about deterrence in two different ways. We developed the wording for these questions ourselves, so no comparisons with other opinion polls are possible. However, we believe these questions word the issue more precisely than the questions taken from other surveys. Given the widespread availability of "life without parole" as an alternative to the death penalty,[33] the first question displayed in Table 3 is perhaps the clearest statement of the deterrence issue as actually faced by researchers and policy makers today. It focuses on the *unique* deterrent effect of the death penalty above and beyond available alternatives of long imprisonment. Only three of our respondents (4.5%) agreed, and none strongly agreed, with the statement, "overall, over the last twenty years, the threat or use of the death penalty in the United States has been a stronger deterrent to homicide than the threat or use of long (or life) prison sentences." Those disagreeing or strongly disagreeing included 92.6% of the respondents, and 96% of those with an opinion.

Responses to the next question indicate that only three respondents felt that the empirical support for the deterrent effects of the death penalty had moderate support; none believed it had strong support. Instead, 94% of the criminologists felt the argument had weak or no support.

The question of reform

Proponents of the death penalty might concur with the critics of the deterrence argument, but say that the lack of a clear deterrent effect is a result of the fact that only a small proportion of those on death row are executed each year, or that the wait on death row between condemnation and execution is too long. Increasing the frequency and celerity of the death penalty could produce a deterrent effect. The experts responding to our survey, however, disagree with such a position. Almost 80% disagree or strongly disagree with the statement, "if the frequency of executions were to increase significantly, more homicides would be deterred than if the current frequency of executions remained relatively stable." As seen in the second portion of Table 4, nearly three quarters (73.2%) of the experts disagreed or strongly disagreed with the position that decreasing the time on death row would deter more homicides. Much of the research that informs these experts' opinions was done with data from the 1930's, 1940's, and 1950's, when the frequency of executions was higher and the average time spent on death row was shorter than it is today. Hence, criminologists do have some research at their disposal that would enable accurate predictions of what would happen if these proposed death penalty reforms were actually enacted.

Support for the brutalization hypothesis

In a final question, the experts were asked how they felt about the so-called "brutalization hypothesis." This argument, supported by some research,[34] suggests that the death penalty tends to devalue human life and sends a message that tells citizens that killing people under some circumstances is appropriate. However, as shown in Table 5, this hypothesis does not have widespread support among the experts. Two-thirds (67.1%) of the respondents either disagree or strongly disagree with the statement, "overall, the presence of the death penalty tends to *increase* a state's murder rate rather than to *decrease* it."

The responses to this item help us address some possible reservations about our overall findings: Is there anti-capital punishment bias among the respondents? Were the responses made based on an understanding of the research or are our respondents merely liberal academics who object to the death penalty on moral grounds and would report opinions that might undermine it, even if the empirical evidence showed otherwise? The responses to the question on brutalization suggest that the answers to these questions are negative. If the respondents simply responded to any question in a way that buttresses the abolitionist position, there should be strong agreement with the notion that the death penalty actually increases the homicide rate, since this is an anti-capital punishment argument. It appears, instead, that the respondents were responding on the grounds we asked—their appraisal of existing research. The brutalization hypothesis, in fact has not been tested very well and the research supporting it remains more suggestive than definitive. As on the other questions, the respondents appear to have reacted to the state of knowledge on this question (as they were instructed), not to personal preferences.

Scholarship and public policy

The results of this project show that there is a wide consensus among America's top criminologists that scholarly research has demonstrated that the death penalty does, and can do, little to reduce rates of criminal violence. Hence, these leading criminologists do not concur with one of the most important public justifications for the death penalty in modern society.

Do politicians and policy makers pay any attention to expert opinions among members or leaders of scholarly societies? There is some evidence in the recent ASC task force panel reports to the Attorney General that they may on some issues.[35] But that task force, while studying a dozen crime control policy options, did not examine the issue of capital punishment. The advice we would offer, reflecting the opinions of the presidents of the major criminological organizations, is to shift public debates about how to reduce criminal violence in America away from the death penalty.

Capital punishment will continue to generate much public debate in the early decades of the twenty-first century and various bodies of opinion will be consulted. One important body of opinion has been revealed by this study. The results show that the question of whether or not the death penalty can reduce criminal violence is—at least for the presidents of the major scholarly societies in criminology—a settled issue. Hopefully this study will provide policy makers with information that might help move political debate beyond "gut" feelings and simplistic demands for the death penalty as a way of "getting tough" on crime. Careful consideration of alternatives can build a public consensus around more effective policies that really hold promise in reducing America's high rates of criminal violence.

Table 1.

Comparison of Responses of Criminologists and General Public to Identical Questions on Deterrence

A. Do you feel that the death penalty acts as a deterrent to the commitment of murder—that it lowers the murder rate, or what?

	Criminology Presidents (%)	Gallup 1985[36] (%)	Gallup 1991[37] (%)
Yes:	11.9	62	51
No:	83.6	31	41
No Opinion:	4.5	7	8
N*	67	1,523	990

B. Abolishing the death penalty (in a particular state) would not have any significant effects on the murder rate (in that state).

	Criminology Presidents (%)	Ellsworth and Ross, 1983[38] (%)
I'm sure it is true	32.8	10.2
I think it's true	53.7	35.8
I have no idea whether it is true or false	10.4	32.6
I think it's false	3.0	18.0
I'm sure it's false	0	3.4
N	67	500

C. Over the years, states which have had the death penalty have had lower murder rates than neighboring states which did not have a death penalty.

	Criminology Presidents (%)	Ellsworth and Ross[39] (%)
I'm sure it is true	0	4.6
I think it's true	6.0	22.4
I have no idea	14.9	6.0
I think it's false	40.3	32.0
I'm sure it's false	38.8	5.0
N	67	500

*N = Number of Respondents

Table 2.

Comparison of Responses of Criminologists (N=67) and Police Chiefs[40] to Same Questions (N=386) (in percents)

A. Politicians support the death penalty as a symbolic way to show they are tough on crime.

	Presidents	Police Chiefs
Totally accurate	38.8	33
Largely accurate	61.2	52
Largely inaccurate	0	10
Totally inaccurate	0	6
Not sure	0	2

B. Debates about the death penalty distract Congress and state legislatures from focusing on real solutions to crime problems.

	Presidents	Police Chiefs
Totally accurate	49.3	11
Largely accurate	37.3	46
Largely inaccurate	11.9	30
Totally inaccurate	0	11
Not sure	1.5	2

C. The death penalty significantly reduces the number of homicides.

	Presidents	Police Chiefs
Totally accurate	0	4
Largely accurate	0	22
Largely inaccurate	41.8	45
Totally inaccurate	52.2	22
Not sure	6.0	7

Table 3.

Responses of Criminologists to General Questions on Deterrence
(N=67) (in percents)

A. Overall, over the last twenty years, the threat or use of the death penalty
in the United States has been a stronger deterrent to homicide than the
threat or use of long (or life) prison sentences.

Strongly agree 0
Agree 4.5
Disagree...43.3
Strongly disagree 49.3
Missing...3.0

B. Overall, how would you evaluate the empirical support for the deterrent
effects of the death penalty?

Strong support...0
Moderate support 4.5
Weak support...44.8
No support...49.3
Missing...1.5

Table 4.

Responses of Criminologists to Belief that Reforms Could Produce a
Deterrent Effect (N=67) (in percents)

A. If the frequency of executions were to increase significantly, more homicides would be deterred than if the current frequency of executions remained relatively stable.

Strongly agree 3.0
Agree 14.9
Disagree...44.8
Strongly disagree..34.3
Missing...3.0

B. The average time on death row between sentence and execution is now
between eight and ten years. If that period was reduced significantly,
there is reason to expect that the death penalty would deter more homicides than it does today.

Strongly agree 4.5
Agree 22.4
Disagree...44.8
Strongly disagree..28.4

Table 5.

Criminologists' Responses to the Brutalization Hypothesis (N=67)
(in percents)

A. Overall, the presence of the death penalty tends to *increase* a state's murder rate rather than to *decrease* it.

Strongly agree 4.5
Agree 23.9
Disagree..52.2
Strongly disagree 14.9
Missing..4.5

Sources

1. David W. Moore, *Majority Advocates Death Penalty for Teenage Killers*, GALLUP POLL MONTHLY, Sept. 1994, at 5.

2. Hugo Adam Bedau, *Retribution and the Theory of Punishment*, 75 J. PHIL. 602 (1978); James O. Finckenauer, *Public Support for the Death Penalty: Retribution as Just Desserts or Retribution as Revenge?*, 5 JUST. Q. 81 (1988).

3. Glenn L. Pierce & Michael L. Radelet, *The Role and Consequences of the Death Penalty in American Politics*, 18 N.Y.U. REV. L. & SOC. CHANGE 711, 715 (1990–91).

4. *See* Stephen B. Bright, *The Politics of Crime and the Death Penalty: Not 'Soft on Crime,' but Hard on the Bill of Rights*, 39 ST. LOUIS U. L.J. 479, 483 (1995).

5. Edwin H. Sutherland, *Murder and the Death Penalty*, 15 J. CRIM. L. & CRIMINOLOGY 522 (1925).

6. *See* James Alan Fox et al., *Death Penalty Opinion in the Post-*Furman *Years*, 18 N.Y.U. REV. L. & SOC. CHANGE 499, 513–14 (1990–91); *see also* William J. Bowers, *Capital Punishment and Contemporary Values: People's Misgivings and the Court's Misperceptions*, 27 L. & SOC'Y REV. 157, 167–71 (1993).

7. *See* Fox et al., *supra* note 6, at 514–15; *see also* Bowers, *supra* note 6, at 163–64.

8. Alec Gallup & Frank Newport, *Death Penalty Support Remains Strong*, GALLUP POLL MONTHLY, June 1991, at 40.

9. RAYMOND PATERNOSTER, CAPITAL PUNISHMENT IN AMERICA 217–45 (1991).

10. Isaac Ehrlich, *The Deterrent Effect of Capital Punishment: A Question of Life and Death*, 65 AM. ECON. REV. 397 (1975).

11. *Id.* at 398.

12. THE DEATH PENALTY IN AMERICA 95 (Hugo Adam Bedau ed., 3rd ed. 1982).

13. Lawrence R. Klein et al., *The Deterrent Effect of Capital Punishment: An Assessment of the Estimates, in* DETERRENCE AND INCAPACITATION: ESTIMATING THE EFFECTS OF CRIMINAL SANCTIONS ON CRIME RATES (Alfred Blumstein et al. eds., 1978).

14. *See, e.g.,* Brian Forst, *Capital Punishment and Deterrence: Conflicting Evidence?*, 74 J. CRIM. L. & CRIMINOLOGY 927 (1983); Gordon P. Waldo, *The Death Penalty and Deterrence: A Review of Recent Research, in* THE MAD, THE BAD, AND THE DIFFERENT (Israel L. Barak-Glantz & C. Ronald Huff eds., 1981).

15. *See, e.g.,* Thomas Sowell, *Death Penalty Is Valid Option,* ST. LOUIS POST DISPATCH, Dec. 12, 1994, at 11C.

16. Stephen K. Layson, *Homicide and Deterrence: A Reexamination of the United States Time-Series Evidence,* 52 S. ECON. J. 68, 80 (1985).

17. *See generally* James Alan Fox & Michael L. Radelet, *Persistent Flaws in Econometric Studies of the Deterrent Effect of the Death Penalty,* 23 LOY. L.A. L. REV. 29 (1989).

18. *See, e.g., Habeas Corpus: Hearings on H.R. 3131 Before the Subcomm. on Civil and Const. Rights of the House Comm. on the Judiciary,* 103rd Cong. 228, 253–55 (1993) (statement of Paul G. Cassell, Associate Professor of Law, University of Utah College of Law).

19. *See, e.g.,* Gallup & Newport, *supra* note 8, at 40; *7 in 10 Favor Death Penalty for Murder,* GALLUP REPORT, Jan.–Feb. 1986, at 10; *Support for the Death Penalty Highest in Half-Century,* GALLUP REPORT, Jan.–Feb. 1986, at 3.

20. *See 7 in 10 Favor Death Penalty for Murder, supra* note 19, at 11–12, 15.

21. *See* Gallup & Newport, *supra* note 8, at 41, 43.

22. Phoebe C. Ellsworth & Lee Ross, *Public Opinion and Capital Punishment: A Close Examination of the Views of Abolitionists and Retentionists,* 29 CRIME & DELINQ. 116 (1983).

23. *Id.* at 151.

24. RICHARD C. DIETER, DEATH PENALTY INFORMATION CENTER, ON THE FRONT LINE: LAW ENFORCEMENT VIEWS ON THE DEATH PENALTY 2 (1995); PETER D. HART RESEARCH ASSOCIATES, INC. STUDY No. 4236 DEATH PENALTY—POLICE CHIEFS (1995) (on file with author).

25. Patrick V. Murphy, *Death Penalty Useless,* USA TODAY, Feb. 23, 1995, at 11A.

26. *See* Klein et al., *supra* note 13, at 336.

27. ENCYCLOPEDIA OF ASSOCIATIONS 10803 (Sandra Jaszczak ed., 31st ed. 1996).

28. *Id.* at 10742.

29. Each organization elects officers, including a president, by a ballot sent to all members. To be elected president, one must generally have high visibility in the field, be well-respected, and have been active in programmatic and organizational activities.

30. ENCYCLOPEDIA OF ASSOCIATIONS, *supra* note 27, at 5334.

31. One of these former presidents is a co-author of this paper (RLA).

32. DIETER, *supra* note 24, at 10 fig. 4, 14–15.

33. *See generally* Julian H. Wright Jr., *Life-Without-Parole: An Alternative to Death or Not Much of a Life at All?,* 43 VAND. L. REV. 529 (1990).

34. William C. Bailey, *Deterrence and the Death Penalty for Murder in Oregon,* 16 WILLAMETTE L. REV. 67, 84–85 & n.36 (1979); William C. Bailey, *Disaggregation in Deterrence and Death Penalty Research: The Case of Murder in*

Chicago, 74 J. CRIM. L. & CRIMINOLOGY 827, 855–58 (1983); William J. Bowers & Glenn L. Pierce, *Deterrence or Brutalization: What Is the Effect of Executions?,* 26 CRIME & DELINQ. 453, 456–59 (1980); John K. Cochran et al., *Deterrence or Brutalization? An Impact Assessment of Oklahoma's Return to Capital Punishment,* 32 CRIMINOLOGY 107, 110–30 (1994).

35. Freda Adler, *Our American Society of Criminology, the World, and the State of the Art—The American Society of Criminology 1995 Presidential Address,* 34 CRIMINOLOGY 1, 2 (1996).

36. *Support for the Death Penalty Highest in Half-Century, supra* note 19, at 6.

37. Gallup & Newport, *supra* note 8, at 41.

38. Ellsworth & Ross, *supra* note 22, at 141. The Ellsworth and Ross question read, "Studies have not found that abolishing the death penalty has any significant effect on the murder rate in a state."

39. *Id.*

40. PETER D. HART RESEARCH ASSOCIATES, INC., *supra* note 24, at 6.

10

Death Is the Most Effective Deterrent

Michael Davis

Michael Davis is senior research associate at the Center for the Study of Ethics in the Professions at the Illinois Institute of Technology. Davis has published many articles, including two dozen on criminal justice, and is the author of the books To Make the Punishment Fit the Crime *and* Justice in the Shadow of Death: Rethinking Capital and Lesser Punishments, *from which this viewpoint is taken.*

Deterrence is central to the debate over the death penalty. Those opposed to the death penalty cite social science statistics to prove that homicide rates are not effected by capital punishment. Those in favor of the death penalty argue that it is common sense that criminals, because they fear death more than any other punishment, will be deterred by the threat of death. Common sense is a better method than social science to determine if capital punishment is a deterrent for three main reasons: social science data are rough and incomplete; there is no adequate social science theory to interpret the data; and the findings from social science have been inconclusive. Common sense proves that the penalty of death is the most effective deterrent.

To deter is to turn away (by fear). To claim that death is the most effective deterrent is to claim that legal provision for a penalty of death *both* a) would (all else equal) turn any potential criminal from a crime if any penalty would *and* b) would (all else equal) turn some potential criminals from some crime when no other penalty would.

When people debate the justification of the death penalty, sooner or later, they almost inevitably argue "deterrence." Those favoring the death penalty argue that death deters better than life imprisonment (or some lesser term); those opposed, that it does not. Deterrence remains central to the debate over the death penalty; other considerations radiate from it like streets leading from a town's center. The argument for the death penalty that relies on deterrence—what I shall call *the argument from deterrence*—may be stated in this way:

Reprinted, by permission, from chapter one of Michael Davis, *Justice in the Shadow of Death: Rethinking Capital and Lesser Punishments* (Lanham, MD: Rowman & Littlefield, 1996), which originally appeared as an article in the Summer 1981 issue of the journal *Social Theory and Practice.*

1. The state should, all else equal, provide as penalty the most effective deterrent among those humanely available;
2. (The penalty of) death is the most effective deterrent (among those humanely available);
3. (The penalty of) death is humanely available;
4. All else is equal (for murder and perhaps for certain other crimes);

So: The state should provide death as penalty for murder (and perhaps for certain other crimes).

This viewpoint's subject is premise 2. I shall argue: that premise 2 requires a method of proof I call "the method of common sense"; that anyone who accepts the criminal law as a reasonable means of controlling certain human behavior ought to accept the method of common sense in the proof of premise 2; and that the method does prove death to be the most effective deterrent among those humanely available. . . .

Deterrence and common sense

Debates over deterrence often go something like this: Those opposed to the death penalty appeal to the statistics of social science to prove that there is no established relation between statutory provisions for death and the actual rate of capital crime. Those favoring the death penalty respond, "So what? We don't need social science. Our claim is just plain common sense." That response earns nothing but unconcealed condescension from death-penalty opponents. To those who appeal to social science, the appeal to common sense sounds old-fashioned and therefore outmoded. Yet the debate over the death penalty has regularly taken this form at least since the French debated abolition in 1791.[1] *Both* appeals are old-fashioned. Some deep misunderstanding divides the two sides, leaving each talking almost entirely to its own.

Consider, for example, what Justice Brennan had to say about the argument from deterrence in a classic 1972 death-penalty case, *Furman v. Georgia.* Brennan's attack (the part of concern here) is clearly against premise 2. The attack has two stages. The first stage treats premise 2 as a claim to be supported by ordinary scientific evidence. There is, he points out, no such evidence. Comparative statistics give no reason to believe death a more effective deterrent than a long prison term.[2] (That is so, but the defense of premise 2 has rarely relied on such empirical evidence, though those attacking the death penalty usually suppose that it should.)

Having thus pushed through the outworks, Brennan reaches the citadel, common sense:

> The States argue, however, that they are entitled to rely upon common human experience, and that experience, they say, supports the conclusion that death must be a more effective deterrent than any less severe punishment. Because people fear death the most, the argument runs, the threat of death must be the greatest deterrent.[3]

Brennan treats this second defense as a continuation of the first (scientific) defense by other means. Though the claim is arguable, he does not deny that people fear death the most (supposing that torture and other inhumane penalties are not among the alternatives). He merely tries to explain why that fear does not appear from the evidence and why, therefore, it is irrelevant. He supposes he must explain away that "common human experience" because he does not know what else to do with it. He has two explanations: *First,* the defense makes an unrealistic assumption about potential criminals:

> [The] argument can only apply to . . . the rational person who will commit a capital crime knowing that the punishment is long-term imprisonment . . . but will not commit the crime knowing that the punishment is death. On the face of it, the assumption that such persons exist is implausible.[4]

Second, Brennan explains, the defense also makes an unrealistic assumption about the legal system:

> Proponents of this argument necessarily admit that its validity depends upon the existence of a system in which the punishment of death is invariably and swiftly imposed. Our system, of course, satisfies neither condition. . . . The risk of death is remote and improbable; in contrast, the risk of long-term imprisonment is near and great. . . . Whatever might be the case were all or substantially all eligible criminals quickly put to death, unverifiable possibilities are an insufficient basis upon which to conclude that the threat of death has any greater deterrent efficacy than the threat of imprisonment.[5]

Brennan is twice mistaken. The argument from deterrence is independent of the assumption that potential criminals calculate risk like graduates of a business school. Defenders need only assume that the threat of death will guide the action of a potential criminal somehow or other. The threat of death may give forbidden acts a special fearfulness that the less calculating appreciate without understanding. The threat of death may reinforce social practices that in turn steer the potential criminal away from even conceiving of the forbidden act. And so on. The argument's defenders have said as much many times.[6]

The argument from deterrence is also independent of the unrealistic assumption that our legal system (or any other) invariably and swiftly imposes death upon those guilty of capital crimes. The argument does perhaps assume that the death penalty is not mandatory upon conviction.— If it were mandatory, a potential criminal could rationally gamble that judge or jury would find him not guilty in order to escape having to condemn him to die.—However, except where there is a mandatory sentence of death (a possibility we may hereafter ignore), the potential criminal should look upon death as a risk to be added to the risk of imprisonment. The possibility of a (nonmandatory) death sentence, however improbable, is no more than one more bad consequence that may follow upon the crime. Where there is no death penalty for murder, he risks imprisonment. Where there is a death penalty for murder, he risks imprisonment or death. As long as death is worse than imprisonment, the risk of death, no matter how much smaller than the risk of imprisonment, adds to the reasons against committing a capital crime. A potential criminal may in fact ignore that risk, but he cannot rationally do so. Thus, Brennan's second explanation returns us to his first, the sense of assuming that the potential criminal will adjust his acts to accord with the threat of punishment (whether he does that consciously or not).

Though Brennan is twice mistaken, it does not much matter. The argument from deterrence does not gain its strength from either of the assumptions that Brennan foists on the defenders or even from the alternatives I mentioned. The argument no more needs armchair social science than it needs comparative statistics. The argument's strength is out of all proportion to the delicate evidence upon which such social science would have to found it. The argument stands like a granite wall set in bedrock: *Because people fear death the most, the threat of death must be the greatest deterrent.* Brennan's attack, like so many before it, rushes past that stronghold chasing a phantom.

All right, you say, let us admit that Brennan has misunderstood the argument from deterrence. How, then, is it to be understood? If premise 2 does not rest on the evidence of social science, on what does it rest? On what *could* it rest? My answer is "common sense" I must now explain how that can be.

Social science or common sense?

Common sense (as I use that term here) does not name a source of knowledge different from that of social science. Common sense is not intuition or revelation. Both common sense and social science draw from the same well of human experience. The difference between them is like that between social science and judicial fact-finding, a difference in what is drawn and how it is drawn, a difference in method of noting and assessing experience. Each method serves certain human interests, but not even the method of social science can serve all. In this section I justify using common sense to establish the deterrent value of penalties. I do that in three steps. First, I describe the method of common sense. Second, I contrast it with the method of social science. And last, I show that, for purposes of criminal law, common-sense conclusions about deterrence serve better than those of social science.

The *method of common sense* is familiar. We ask ourselves what we would do if thus-and-so were true, what we would think if such-and-such happened, and so on. We do not have to pump the world for information. As long as we ask the right questions, the answers readily pour from us. Who is this "us"? What is it we do? This "us" is all of us, more or less, the same "us" that does science or follows rules. Common sense is *common* because we all share in it. But common sense is *sense* only because what we share is rationality. Rationality (as I use the term here) includes reason, that is, the capacity to observe, generalize, hypothesize, infer, plan, predict, and do those other calculated acts characteristic of both scientific research and everyday life. Rationality is, however, not only reasoning. The man who methodically sets about to maim himself with no further object is, though perhaps technically gifted and ultimately satisfied, not rational. He is mad. Besides reason, rationality includes certain basic evaluations, for example, that (all else equal) loss of limb, life, or freedom is to be avoided. What we, as rational persons, do is reason from those basic evaluations. That is the method of common sense.

The method is fallible. You and I make mistakes. The more complicated the reasoning, the more likely that we will err. We are well advised to compare our basic evaluations with those of others to make sure we have them right, and also well advised to open our reasoning to public examination. Multiplying reasoners, though it cannot make error impossible, can at least make it unlikely.

Though fallible, the method of common sense is neither unreliable nor "subjective." Consider an analogy. You and I both speak English. Sometimes what we say comes out gibberish. Sometimes we are mistaken about what we can correctly say. Our speech sometimes benefits from the criticism of others. Nevertheless, we are generally right about what is correct English. While the capacity to speak English does not guarantee performance in every case, it does guarantee it in general. Being a native speaker makes one an authority on what a native speaker would say. Being rational is a capacity like being an English speaker. The rational person's knowledge of what is rational is as reliable as her knowledge of her own language; rationality itself is no more "subjective" than language is. The method of common sense works well for the same reason the linguist finds that the best way to learn a language is to ask a native speaker what she would say. The rational person is in the same position with respect to what is rational that the native speaker is with respect to what it would be correct to say.

The particular truths of common sense are, therefore, at once conceptual and contingent. They are conceptual because they follow from premises all rational persons share. The premises include (beside the basic evaluations already mentioned) such facts about ourselves as everyone knows, for example, that we (both you and I) may be injured, that we plan, that we are rational, and that we may act upon our plans. The truths of common sense are nevertheless contingent insofar as the premises and principles of reasoning are no more necessary *a priori* [beforehand] than the principle of induction or the deep structure of human language. We could, it seems, have been beings who, though rational (in the sense explained above), would not come to know that others could suffer injuries, that we could plan, that we were rational, and so on.[7] The method of common sense yields knowledge of rational agents only insofar as we are rational agents and only because rational agents are what they are.

Because people fear death the most, the threat of death must be the greatest deterrent.

The *method of social science* is to assume nothing about those to be studied, to collect relevant data, and to draw only such conclusions as the data support. The social scientist pretends to be an outsider, to know nothing about the subject of research except what he culls from his data. While he may use his own experience to help plan research or formulate hypotheses, he must treat that experience as mere hunch or subjective impression. That pretence is what is supposed to make the method "value free." The collected data consist of records of "behavior," that is, of records of acts and events described as an outsider would describe them insofar as that is practical. The social scientist may simply gather existing records of behavior (police records of suicides, homicides, and so on) or may actively generate data by taking surveys or staging experiments. Because the data are in terms of behavior, the conclusions drawn from the data must be too. Social science (so described) is merely a science of behavior. Its standard of proof is both difficult to satisfy and highly specialized.

I do not claim this description of social science accurately describes social science generally. While a positivist might not object to that calumny, all I claim is that I have accurately described the method of social science implicit in much of what the opponents of the death penalty say. Consider, for example, the following passage from H.L.A. Hart's discussion of the argument from deterrence.

> If we turn from the statistical evidence to the other "evidence," the latter really amounts simply to the alleged truism that men fear death more than any other penalty, and that therefore it must be a stronger deterrent than imprisonment. . . .[8]

The use of the word "scientific" or "empirical," like Hart's contrast between statistical evidence and the (scare-quoted) "evidence" of common sense, is a sure sign that the special method of social science is being treated as the only appropriate one.

The method of social science is, however, only appropriate for some questions. For example, suppose that you make "Brand X" bagels and want to increase sales. You want people to ask for your bagels, put money on the counter, and walk off, bagels in hand. You do not care why they do it as long as they do; you would as soon have them do it for bad reasons as for good. You do not even care whether the buyers would have to be mad to pay your price so long as you can get them to do it. You are concerned only with getting a certain behavior. If that is all you are concerned about, then the method of social science may be just what you need.

Suppose instead that you are a linguist about to study a human language. To be a linguist is to assume that those you study have a capacity for language. To go somewhere to study a certain language is to assume that the language spoken there is one you can learn. The linguist is never altogether an outsider. Because she knows a good deal about her own language (as well as those she has already studied as a linguist), she begins work on her next language with at least one foot in the door. Pretending otherwise would be a waste of time. Perhaps the method of social science would, in time, approximate the results that the linguist's method gets much sooner. Whether that is actually so is a tangled question in philosophy of language that I need not unravel here. My point is simply that, whatever might in time be possible, using the method of social science instead of the linguist's method would be a waste of time. If what you want is to learn the language as soon as possible, the method of social science is not what you need. What you need is to ask a native speaker what he would say.

Which method is preferable for deciding the deterrent value of penalties? The method of social science may at first seem preferable. After all, are we not, like the bagel-maker, concerned only with getting certain behavior? Do we care why people obey the law so long as they do? If raising the penalty for breaking a certain law would mean fewer crimes, would we not have a reason to raise the penalty? And if raising the penalty had no visible effect, could we justify the higher penalty? The method of social science seemingly tells us just what we need to know. The method of common sense seems, in contrast, to offer only (in Justice Brennan's words) "unverifiable possibilities" or (in Hart's words) "alleged truisms." Seeming, unfortunately, does not make it so. The method of social science seems preferable only while we see the criminal law as nothing more than a system for controlling behavior generally. The instant we notice that it is more than that, that it is a particular system for controlling a special kind of behavior, social science no longer seems preferable to common sense.

The criminal law and rational action

The criminal law is a system for controlling the acts of rational agents by making certain acts rationally less appealing. Criminal laws differ from laws that simply provide for official action if something happens (for example, a health law requiring quarantine of anyone with contagious tuberculosis). The criminal law is supposed to consist of rules that a potential criminal can follow or not as she chooses. Every criminal law has a penalty for its violation. The penalty is supposed to give the potential criminal a reason to follow the rule. The potential criminal is supposed to be someone who, though perhaps immoral and heartless, can still recognize the penalty as a reason for not violating the law. If we do not think of the potential criminal as someone who can be guided by law and penalty, we are at a loss to justify any punishment whatever. We can, of course, justify something like punishment, for example, sending the lawbreaker to a mental hospital as if she were insane, or caging her as if she were a wild animal, or disposing of her altogether as if she were a rabid dog. We cannot, however, justify fining a lawbreaker, warning her, or locking her up for a set time only to turn her loose again whatever she was or has become. The criminal law makes no sense unless we suppose the potential criminal to be more or less rational. On that at least, both deterrence theorists and retributive theorists have always agreed.

Indeed, even reform theorists agree that the criminal law makes that supposition. It is for just that supposition that they criticize the criminal law. Beneath debate of the death penalty swim luminous doubts about the criminal law as we know it. The same statistics that fail to show death to deter better than long imprisonment also fail to show long imprisonment to deter better than brief imprisonment. I shall not fish up those doubts here. The purpose of this viewpoint is to clarify the argument from deterrence. Both those who make the argument and most of those who attack it accept the criminal law as is, agree that certain penalties deter better than others, and disagree only about whether death deters better than any alternative penalty. While they do not think social order depends entirely on the criminal law, they do think that the criminal law makes a substantial contribution. Still, since doubts are easier to extinguish than to evade, let me briefly make four points to clarify how relatively uncontroversial should be the claim that the potential criminal is rational.

First, the claim is not that all *lawbreakers* are rational. We may admit that some lawbreakers are insane (or otherwise incompetent). The admission merely commits us to controlling those lawbreakers differently than the rest. We commit ourselves to excluding them (more or less) from criminal justice. . . . The sane may be punished; the insane may not. We need not claim that rational persons constitute any particular percentage of potential or actual lawbreakers.

The method of social science has no monopoly on knowledge about what rational agents will do.

Second, we need not claim that people have "free will." We may admit (for what it's worth) that we are all prey to the dance of atoms, that the perfect physicist could predict our every motion, or that society makes us what we are. We need claim only that the prospect of penalty is a factor that may help to guide a potential criminal away from this or that prohibited act.

Third, we need not claim that only the prospect of penalty keeps rational persons from committing crimes. We may admit that there are other good reasons to obey the law (for example, the opinion of one's neighbor or the lack of opportunity or motive). We may also admit that habit, superstition, awe of authority, and other blind sentiments help to keep us law-abiding even when we do not stop to think. The judge does not wear his long black robe in vain. We may even accept the distinction between good citizen and potential criminal. The good citizen would obey the law (for good reason or from blind sentiment) even absent a penalty for disobeying. The potential criminal would disobey if there were not some penalty (and some chance of suffering it). Though the distinction between good citizen and potential criminal is probably relative to the law in question, we may admit that any society with many potential criminals will have trouble keeping order. What we must claim is that a rational person *could* commit a crime. The proof of that is easy enough. We have only to examine ourselves to find someone who would, though rational, break the law *under easily imaginable circumstances* if either the penalty itself or the risk of suffering it were not sufficiently high. Some of us, perhaps, have even contemplated murder.

Fourth, we need not claim that a criminal *act* must be rational for the agent to be subject to punishment. Rational agents sometimes act irrationally; that is, they do what they have good reason not to do, because they did not stop to think, because they misjudged the chance of capture, or because they did not appreciate the penalty. Such persons remain fit subjects of punishment because they should not have done the act even if there were no penalty (or no chance of suffering it). They cannot complain because *they* miscalculated. "Okay, I made a mistake: I should have known I couldn't get away with that!" is an admission of guilt, not a plea of excuse. Such miscalculation is not to be confused with temporary inability to act rationally (for example, when acting under posthypnotic suggestion) or reduced ability to reason (for example, when acting under extreme provocation). Such inability constitutes full or partial excuse exactly insofar as it could lead anyone, good citizen as well as potential criminal, to commit the crime.

Since the criminal law presupposes that the potential criminal is rational, it presupposes as well that we have much in common with him. He shares with us certain basic evaluations, and he can reason as we do. We can assess options as he can, plan as he can, and even act as he can. We may reasonably ask ourselves what we would do if such-and-such and expect an answer that is also the answer of the potential criminal. To accept the criminal law as a reasonable means of social control is then to presuppose that we are in a position to use the method of common sense to determine the deterrent value of penalties. Rationality is itself the "common human experience" upon which the argument from deterrence is supposed to rely. The only question remaining is whether we should prefer the method of common sense to the method of social science. There are, I think, at least four reasons why we should:

First, social science has nothing conclusive to report. The findings of social science to date—"no established correlation between death penalty and murder rate"—are consistent with any findings common sense is likely to make.[9] The inability of social science to establish a correlation does not entail the inability of other methods of discovery to do better. The method of social science has no monopoly on knowledge about what rational agents will do.

Second, social science is admittedly working under conditions unfavorable to it. The data are rough and incomplete, consisting as much of police reports of crime as of judicial sentences and official announcements of executions. Categories of crime vary from jurisdiction to jurisdiction, from period to period. The rate at which crimes get reported varies as well. There have been few surveys and no controlled experiments. Statistical analysis requires controversial assumptions about the independence of variables.[10]

Third, social scientists are not now in position to interpret better data even if they had it. There is no adequate theory of society. Social scientists would not know how to distinguish the effect on their data produced by a change in statutory penalty from the effect produced by a change in rates of reporting crime, by a change in knowledge of penalty, by a change in the pool of potential criminals, by a change in success of prosecution, or by a change in any number of other factors. Social scientists do not even know all the factors to check for. All they know is how to start searching out such things and, even so, they do not know how long the search will take.

Last, there is no reason to believe that, when social scientists have better data and are in position to control for extraneous factors, they will come to conclusions about rational agents inconsistent with those that the method of common sense yields now. An inconsistency between the method of social science and that of common sense is no more to be expected than an inconsistency between the method of social science and that of the linguist. The method of common sense is, after all, conceptual.

The most the method of social science could show is that potential law-breakers are never rational (an unlikely discovery) or that the pool of potential criminals is much smaller than commonly supposed (a less unlikely discovery). No such discovery would undermine the claims of common sense about what it is rational to do, though it would make those claims of less practical importance. Social science does have a special place in the debate over the death penalty. But that place is premise 4, not premise 2. The discoveries of social science cannot affect the findings of common sense concerning what would deter rational agents.

When we consider how little the method of social science has to offer, we must conclude that the method would have no appeal here were it not for a misunderstanding of the method of common sense. I have, I hope, now cleared up that misunderstanding. If so, we are ready to examine the defense of premise 2 ("Because people fear death the most, the threat of death is the greatest deterrent"). If I have not yet cleared up that misunderstanding, perhaps the following will. What better way to see that the method of common sense works than to see it at work?

Common sense on death

In this section, I apply the method of common sense to the defense of premise 2. The method applies to people only insofar as they are rational agents (just as the linguist's method applies to people only insofar as they are speakers of the language under study). I must therefore restate the defense of premise 2 so that it is explicitly an argument about rational agents. Here is that restatement:

2a. Rational agents fear their own death more than any other evil (that is, any rational agent would prefer any other evil if given a choice between it and death);[11]
2b. If rational agents most fear a certain evil, they would (all else equal) do their best to avoid it (that is, each rational agent would try to avoid that evil where he would try to avoid every other and also sometimes where he would not try to avoid every other);
2c. If rational agents would do their best to avoid an evil, making that evil the penalty for a crime would (all else-equal) turn each rational agent from that crime if any penalty would and would (all else equal) turn some rational agents from that crime even if no other penalty would;
2d. If making an evil the penalty for a crime would have that effect, that penalty is the most effective deterrent;

So: Death is the most effective deterrent.

The defense is now an argument about rational agents, not actual people. The argument is valid. Is it sound? Premises 2b and 2d are unobjectionable. Premise 2b is true because (all else equal) suffering an evil that one could avoid without suffering one as bad or worse would be irrational. Premise 2d simply restates the definition of "the most effective deterrent" given above. But while premises 2b and 2d seem unobjectionable, premises 2a and 2c do not. Let us now consider what objections might be made to them and how good those objections are, beginning with premise 2a.

The first objection to premise 2a is that, as stated, it is false. Death is not the greatest evil. Death combined with any other evil is worse than death alone. A rational agent would, for example, prefer immediate death to death by slow, painful torture. More important, a rational agent may prefer death to some evils not involving death. We have only to think of the living dead of Dachau: on one side, hard labor, beatings, hunger, hopeless waiting, the steady contraction of humanity; on the other, quick death on an electrified fence. Who would say that those who chose the fence acted irrationally? Here rational people may disagree about what it is better to do. What, then, are we to make of the claim that rational agents fear their own death more than any other evil?[12]

Obviously, the claim must have a limiting context. The alternative to death cannot include death by slow, painful torture, confinement in a concentration camp, or any other radically inhumane punishment. That, indeed, is the context in which debate over the death penalty goes on. The alternatives to death range only from several years to life in a relatively humane prison. We may, then, escape this first objection simply by rewriting premise 2a to make that context explicit:

2a'. Rational agents fear their own death more than any other evil *humanely available as penalty.*

(Rewriting premise 2a in this way will, of course, mean that the conclusion will have to be rewritten accordingly; hence, the second set of parentheses in my initial statement of premise 2.)

There is another objection to premise 2a. We may put it this way: Is it irrational to prefer death to life in prison? Arguably not. Death, at least, is the end of trouble. Life in prison is an indefinite childhood under harsh rules, in bad company, and without privacy, family, or future. Consider how you would choose if you had two lives before you: a life of thirty years ending with death by electrocution; or the same life until age thirty followed by fifty years more, all in prison. Are you sure you would not choose death at thirty? Is there any decisive reason why you should not? Surely (the objection concludes), here too rational agents may disagree about which to choose.

This second objection is well-founded but beside the point. The objection is well-founded because common sense has little to say about comparative value. The only settled cases are extreme. It would, for example, certainly be irrational (all else equal) to prefer death to a pin prick. Every rational agent would agree that the mild pain of an instant is the lesser evil. The problem here is that we are not comparing a great evil with a small one. We are comparing two great evils, death and life-long loss of freedom. Common sense does not say which to prefer. A rational agent may prefer either. The objection is nevertheless beside the point because we should not be comparing these two evils. Death has a property that life in prison does not: finality. The objection presents life in prison as if the whole fifty years were as final as death. The fifty years in prison are, of course, not final until the last year is served. In the meantime, the prisoner might escape, die, be pardoned, or in some other way not serve out her term. The same, it must be observed, is not true of death. The sentence of death, executed in an instant, is thereafter final.

That observation, though often made, is as often misunderstood. Thus, Brennan says:

> The unusual severity of death is manifested most clearly in its finality and enormity. Death, in these respects, is in a class by itself. . . . Death forecloses even the possibility [of regaining the right to have rights].[13]

The severity of death as a penalty is not, as Brennan says, merely "manifested" in its finality. The finality is almost all there is to death. Take that away, and the "enormity" disappears, too. A little science fiction should make this clear. Imagine a world where it is possible to put a person in a box that suspends his mental activity while permitting his body to age normally and his mental activity to resume once he has left the box (if he leaves the box before his natural death). The criminal penalties in that world, let us suppose, include (beside death and imprisonment as we know them) the novel penalty of suspension of mental activity for life. Obviously, choosing death over suspension would (all else equal) not be rational. Suspension is the rational choice because the only difference between suspension and death is that suspension holds out the hope of pardon, parole, or other clemency while death does not. Is it not equally obvious, then, that prison would have to be a relatively comfortable place before choosing it over suspension could be rational? Insofar as prison is bearable only because it holds out the hope of coming to an end, suspension is preferable, holding out the hope without the burden.

This observation suggests yet another objection to premise 2a, the last I shall consider here: Even if we compare the penalty of death (remembering its finality) with the penalty of life in prison (remembering its tentativeness), we cannot conclude that preferring death to prison is irrational. We could, perhaps, draw that conclusion if the world were somewhat different—if, that is, prisons today were the reformatories described in our high-school civics texts. One would, indeed, have to be irrational to prefer death to a gentle detention hardly worse overall than a pin prick. However, prisons today, though varying widely, are never that gentle, and the worst are terrifying. A prisoner may have to live in an overcrowded cell, eat bad food, and do hard, boring labor. He may live in fear that the guards will torture him, that his fellow prisoners will rape him, or that he will be caught in a war between prison gangs. Life in prison can (so the objection runs) be lonely, grim, futile, oppressive, and ultimately crushing. What does it matter that the prisoner might get out some day if that day is at least years away and might well never arrive?[14] The enormity of death hardly exceeds the enormity of such imprisonment.

This last objection, like the one before it, is at once well-founded and beside the point. The objection is well-founded because choosing death instead of prison is not always irrational, even taking into account the tentativeness of prison. The objection is nevertheless beside the point because what makes prison a lesser penalty than death is just that a prisoner *can* choose death instead of prison while the dead can*not* choose prison instead of death. The finality of death cuts off choice; the tentativeness of prison does not. If a prisoner comes to prefer death to prison, he can (in any ordinary prison) find a way to kill himself (or at least to get himself killed). He therefore has a guarantee that being sent to prison will never be worse than being put to death.[15] Death is his benchmark, the known position from which he can survey life. A rational agent most fears the penalty of death not because he most fears death itself, but because the penalty of death takes from him something no other (humane) penalty can. Any (humane) penalty other than death leaves him two options, that penalty or death, but the penalty of death leaves him to choose between death and death. Any rational person would (all else equal) prefer to have more choice than that.

We should, then, rewrite premise 2a′ to make clear that our concern is not death itself but the *penalty* of death:

> 2a″. Rational agents fear *the penalty of* death more than any other evil humanely available as penalty.

(Rewriting premise 2a′ in this way will, of course, mean another rewriting of the conclusion; hence, the first set of parentheses in the original premise 2.)

Premise 2a (now 2a″) is therefore unobjectionable after all. What of premise 2c ("If rational agents would do their best to avoid a certain evil, threatening that evil as penalty for a crime would turn each rational agent from that crime if any penalty would and would turn some rational agents from that crime even if no other penalty would")? There are two objections: one concerns what the potential criminal *can* appreciate (her capacities), the other, what she *would* appreciate (her performance). I shall discuss the objections in that order.

The *objection from capacity* might be put this way: The threat of death is too remote to be distinguished from the threat of life imprisonment. Even a rational agent can, it seems, handle only so much information, can make only so many discriminations, and so cannot be expected to tune his acts as finely as the legislature can tune its penalties. At the moment before he acts, the potential criminal has to take into account the chances of capture, indictment, and conviction, the vagaries of sentencing, the hope of appeal, pardon, or parole, the possibility of escape, and so on. The distinction between life imprisonment and death *must* (so the objection runs) sink from sight in such a welter of considerations, the inevitable consequence of any system of criminal justice. If life imprisonment would not turn the potential criminal from his crime, neither would death. The potential criminal is, under the circumstances, incapable of seeing the distinction.

Death has a property that life in prison does not: finality.

This objection must be understood within the context of the criminal law. Gradation of penalty is essential to that law. Every system of criminal law today makes distinctions like that between one-year imprisonment and two, one-to-ten years imprisonment and one-to-twenty, one-to-twenty years imprisonment and life. The lower penalty is assigned to the less serious crime. The gradation of penalty is supposed to give the potential criminal a reason to prefer the lesser of two crimes should she have the opportunity to choose between the lesser and the greater. The distinction between life imprisonment and death is one gradation among many, but it is *not* like these others. The other distinctions are distinctions of degree. The distinction between life imprisonment and death is more like a distinction in order of magnitude. The penalty of death is, as explained above, necessarily worse than life imprisonment (no matter how bad life in prison is in fact), because the penalty of death takes from the convicted criminal the power to choose between death and any number of years in prison. To suppose that such a distinction *must* sink from sight is, it seems to me, either to call into question all gradation of penalty or to promise to justify gradation of penalty without deterrence.[16] At least three reasons, each sufficient, require us to reject that supposition and to maintain that some potential criminals can sometimes make the distinction between life imprisonment and death when deciding to commit a crime:

First, the distinction between life imprisonment and death is not always a fine distinction. To the criminal who is serving a life sentence, for example, the distinction between a *second* life sentence and a death sentence would, of course, be as crude as can be. To argue that no potential criminal could make that distinction seems (to turn Justice Brennan's phrase against him) "on the face . . . implausible." Indeed, it is inconsistent with what we, as potential criminals, know we can do.

A rational agent most fears the penalty of death not because he most fears death itself, but because the penalty of death takes from him something no other (humane) penalty can.

Second, the distinction between life imprisonment and death is cruder than distinctions we make all the time amid a storm of considerations no worse than that which might toss a potential criminal. Think what you take into account, for example, when deciding to cancel a life-insurance policy, when choosing between buying a house and renting an apartment, or when considering several job offers. The objection must either portray us as unable to make the fine distinctions necessary for the long-term planning we in fact do or exclude us from the class of potential criminals. Either way, the objection would require us to suppose what we know to be false.

Third, a lawbreaker incapable of making the distinction between life imprisonment and death when deciding to commit a crime would (all else equal) not be a criminal at all. Anyone so feeble-minded (or so steadily and irresistibly preoccupied) that he *could not* take into account that distinction would also be incapable of taking into account most or all gradations of penalty within the criminal law. He would be deaf to its threats. He would not be insane; nor would he necessarily be incompetent in the strict sense. He might be able to manage his everyday life satisfactorily. He would nevertheless be someone to be excluded from criminal justice. His breaking any important law would show his bad character. His inability to distinguish one penalty from another would show him to be someone who might commit several crimes if he committed one and the worst crime as easily as a bad one. He would be a dangerous animal. There would be nothing to do with him but lock him up in some "place of safety," keeping him there until he was no longer dangerous. The objection from capacity assimilates all persons potentially guilty of a capital crime to this special case. The objection leads to an absurdity.

The second objection to premise 2c, *the objection from performance,* is that though some potential criminals may in fact be capable of making the distinction between life imprisonment and death when deciding to commit a crime, there is no reason to believe any *ever* would. The objection must (as an objection to premise 2c) take this extreme form. "Often" or "usually" will not do. If there were only one case where (all else equal) a potential criminal would exercise his capacity to make that distinction and would be turned from a crime because he did not want to risk the death penalty, but would not be turned from the crime by any lesser penalty, the death penalty would (by definition) deter more effectively than any other and premise 2 would be secure.

We cannot, however, respond to the objection by fetching such a case. That would take us beyond the method of common sense (take us, that is, from what everyone knows to what some are privileged to find out). Nor can we respond that the objection makes such an extreme claim that it is unlikely to be true, that a claim's being unlikely is a reason for believing otherwise, and that therefore there is a reason to believe that potential criminals would sometimes distinguish between life imprisonment and death and act accordingly. Such a response is as certain as the probabilities upon which it rests. If the probability is ordinary probability, it is subject to change and so not something all rational persons would agree about. We would again have stepped beyond common sense. If, on the other hand, the probability is somehow conceptually necessary, it would be necessary to explain how that can be.

Common sense provides another response (dependent only on what we mean by "capacity"): Claiming that there is often a slip between capacity and performance is one thing; claiming that there always *would* be is quite another. The former claim might well be true, but the latter is *necessarily* false. To talk of a capacity to do *x* (in certain circumstances) that has yet to be realized makes sense. A startling series of misfortunes might cause such a state of affairs. To talk of the same capacity as one that never *will* be realized, though raising problems of proof, still seems to make sense. To talk this way would be to project that startling series of misfortunes forward until the end of time. But to talk about the same capacity as one that never *would* be realized is fundamentally different. To talk about a capacity to do *x* that never would be realized is to talk about a capacity to do *x* that is *not* a capacity to do *x*. The objection from performance relies upon that contradiction.

Notes

I read the first draft of this before the Philosophy Colloquium, Illinois State University, 13 September 1978 and parts of the second and third sections of a later draft before a session of the Conference on Capital Punishment, Atlanta, Georgia, 19 April 1980. I should like to thank those present at the two readings for many helpful comments. I should also like to thank Nelson Potter and certain anonymous referees at *Ethics* for their detailed criticism of the penultimate draft.

1. Finn Hornum, "Two Debates: France, 1791; England, 1956," in *Capital Punishment*, ed. Thorsten Sellin (New York: Harper & Row, 1967), 62–64, 68–69.

2. *Furman v. Georgia*, 408 U.S. 238, 92 S. Ct. 2726 (1972), 301–303.

3. *Furman v. Georgia*, 301.

4. *Furman v. Georgia*, 302.

5. *Furman v. Georgia*, 302.

6. See, for example, Ernest van den Haag, "On Deterrence and the Death Penalty," *Ethics* 78 (July 1968); 280–289, or John Stuart Mill, "Speech in Favor of Capital Punishment," in *Philosophy of Law*, ed. Joel Feinberg and Hyman Gross (Encino, California: Dickenson Publishing Company, 1975), 620–621. If some of these "sociological" defenses seem to appeal to so-called "non-deterrent preventive effects" (for example, reenforcing social practices), I can only say that there is nothing in the "sociological" form of the argument from deterrence to require the fear of death to operate through any particular mechanism. For a strong attack on van den Haag's (and so on Mill's) statistical argument, see Hugo Adam Bedau, "The Death Penalty as Deterrent—Argument and Evidence," *Ethics* 81 (April 1972): 205–217. For an attack on van den Haag's betting argument, see David A. Conway, "Capital Punishment and Deterrence," *Philosophy and Public Affairs* 3 (Summer 1974): 431–443. Such attacks make clear how delicate the "sociological" arguments are (and how easy it is to confuse them with the argument from common sense) while leaving the argument from common sense untouched.

7. Bernard Gert has argued that the content of rationality is a good deal less contingent than I have made it out to be here. I find his argument at least tempting. See his *The Moral Rules* (Harper Torchbooks: New York, 1973), 23–25 and 164–171.

8. H.L.A. Hart, "Murder and the Principles of Punishment: England and the United States," *Northwestern Law Review* 52 (September 1957): 458. If this quotation leaves any doubt about whether Hart believes the *"alleged* truisms" of common sense to be at all plausible, the context does not.

9. Compare *Furman v. Georgia*, 456–458. The Supreme Court's discussions of the statistical evidence (not only this one discussion but those of all the justices in *Furman*) are, compared to Hart's, so sloppy as to be almost embarrassing to read.

10. For an interesting description of the problems associated with such data, even within a single state, see Hugo Adam Bedau, *Death Is Different* (Boston: Northeastern University Press, 1987), 195–216.

11. By "fear" I mean a recognition that a certain state, event, or outcome is positively undesirable, dangerous, or otherwise something to be avoided because of what it is. Fear (in this sense) does not necessarily involve agitation, panic, or any other distress beyond the mere apprehension of the possibility of suffering what one does not want to suffer. The expression in parentheses is, then, supposed to be a paraphrase of premise 2a. The argument from deterrence, as I understand it, is primarily a conceptual

argument, not a psychological or sociological argument. It is important to keep the human's fear (which belongs to premise 4) distinct from the rational agent's fear (which belongs here in premise 2).

12. Rational people also disagree about whether their own death or that of someone they care about—a parent, friend, or child—would be worse. I ignore this sort of disagreement here not because I suppose people to be egoists generally but because the question before us, the effectiveness of death as a penalty, does not implicate other people directly. No humane system of punishment has open to it the choice of putting someone to death or punishing him in some way through those he cares about. In a humane system of punishment, vicarious punishment is always marginal, involving minor crimes and light penalties.

13. *Furman,* 289–290. Brennan, it should be noted, overstates his point. Even the dead have some rights, for example, the right to a decent burial, the right to have their will carried out, and the right to survival of an action in tort. Whatever the death penalty does deprive one of, it does not deprive one of the right to have rights.

14. For a helpful discussion of the problems that a rational person may face when trying to choose between death and a set of relatively unsatisfactory prospects, see Richard B. Brandt, "The Morality and Rationality of Suicide," in *A Handbook for the Study of Suicide,* ed. Seymour Perlin (New York: Oxford University Press, 1975), 61–76. For an analysis of what makes death an evil similar to the one I give here, see L.S. Summer, "A Matter of Life and Death," *Nous* 10 (May 1976): 153–163. I came upon Summer's article only after I had completed the first draft of the paper out of which this chapter grew. The independence of our work provides additional support for our common conclusion.

15. This is not, as Justice Brennan would perhaps think, a question of rights. There is no legal right to kill oneself, much less a legal right to get oneself killed. The availability of death is merely a fact about the regime of most prisons, a fact that perhaps cannot be changed without invading the few legal rights prisoners have, but a mere fact all the same. My point about choosing death has nothing directly to do with Brennan's point about "the right to have rights."

16. Even a retributivist cannot, I believe, justify the schedule of penalties without appeal to deterrence. To say this is not, let me add, to say that retributive theory is just a confused form of the utilitarian theory of punishment. I certainly would not say that. For my reasons, see chapter 12 of my *Justice in the Shadow of Death: Rethinking Capital and Lesser Punishments* (Roman and Littlefield Publishers, Inc., 1996) and my *To Make the Punishment Fit the Crime* (Boulder: Westview Press, 1992), chapter 4.

Organizations to Contact

The editors have compiled the following list of organizations concerned with the issues debated in this book. The descriptions are derived from materials provided by the organizations. All have publications or information available for interested readers. The list was compiled on the date of publication of the present volume; the information provided here may change. Be aware that many organizations take several weeks or longer to respond to inquiries, so allow as much time as possible.

Amnesty International-USA (AI)
Program to Abolish the Death Penalty
322 Eighth Ave., 10th Fl., New York, NY 10001
(212) 633-4280 • fax: (212) 627-1451
e-mail: mundies@aiusa.org • web address: www.amnesty-usa.org/abolish/

Amnesty International's Program to Abolish the Death Penalty seeks, in the long term, to abolish the death penalty worldwide. In the short term, the program seeks to progressively decrease the use of the death penalty and to increase the number of U.S. states and nations that have removed the death penalty from their legal codes. It publishes the reports *The Death Penalty: List of Abolitionist and Retentionist Countries* and *Facts and Figures on the Death Penalty* several times a year.

Catholics Against Capital Punishment (CACP)
PO Box 3125, Arlington, VA 22203-8125
phone and fax: (301) 652-1125
e-mail: cacp@bellatlantic.net
web address: www2.dcci.com/ltlflwr/CACP.html

Catholics Against Capital Punishment is a national advocacy organization that works to abolish the death penalty in the United States. CACP was founded in 1992 to promote greater awareness of Catholic Church teachings that characterize capital punishment as inappropriate and unacceptable in today's world. It publishes *CACP News Notes* four to six times a year.

Death Penalty Information Center (DPIC)
1320 18th St. NW, 5th Fl., Washington, DC 20036
(202) 293-6970 • fax: (202) 822-4787
e-mail: dpic@essential.org • web address: www.justicefellowship.org

DPIC researches how the public views the death penalty. The center opposes capital punishment, believing it is discriminatory, excessively costly, and may result in the execution of innocent persons. It publishes numerous reports, such as *Millions Misspent: What Politicians Don't Say About the High Costs of the Death Penalty; Innocence and the Death Penalty: Assessing the Danger of Mistaken Executions;* and *With Justice for Few: The Growing Crisis in Death Penalty Representation.*

The Friends Committee to Abolish the Death Penalty (FCADP)
3721 Midvale Ave., Philadelphia, PA 19129
(215) 951-0330 • fax: (215) 951-0342
e-mail: fcadp@aol.com • web address: www.quaker.org/fcadp/

The Friends Committee to Abolish the Death Penalty is a national Quaker organization that was established in 1993. FCADP publishes a quarterly newsletter, the *Quaker Abolitionist.*

Justice Fellowship
PO Box 16069, Washington, DC 20041-6069
(703) 904-7312 • fax: (703) 478-9679
web address: www.justicefellowship.org

The Justice Fellowship is a national criminal justice reform organization that advocates victims' rights, alternatives to prison, and community involvement in the criminal justice system. It aims to make the criminal justice system more consistent with biblical teachings on justice. It does not take a position on the death penalty, but it publishes the pamphlet *Capital Punishment: A Call to Dialogue.*

Lincoln Institute for Research and Education
1001 Connecticut Ave. NW, Suite 1135, Washington, DC 20036
(202) 223-5112

The institute is a conservative think tank that studies public policy issues affecting the lives of African Americans, including the issue of the death penalty, which it favors. It publishes the quarterly *Lincoln Review.*

National Criminal Justice Reference Service (NCJRS)
U.S. Department of Justice
PO Box 6000, Rockville, MD 20849-6000
(800) 851-3420 • (301) 519-5212
e-mail: askncjrs@ncjrs.org • web address: www.ncjrs.org

NCJRS is an international clearinghouse that provides information and research about criminal justice. It works in conjunction with the National Institute of Justice and the Office of Juvenile Justice. NCJRS publishes various reports and journals pertaining to the criminal justice system.

National Legal Aid and Defender Association (NLADA)
1625 K St. NW, 8th Fl., Washington, DC 20006
(202) 452-0620
e-mail: info@nlada.org • web address: www.nlada.org

NLADA acts as an information clearinghouse for organizations that provide legal aid to the poor and advocates high-quality legal services for the indigent. The association publishes materials to assist legal-services organizations and distributes reports by death penalty opponents.

Bibliography

Books

Robert M. Baird and Stuart E. Rosenbaum — *Punishment and the Death Penalty: The Current Debate.* Amherst, NY: Prometheus Books, 1995.

Hugo Adam Bedau — *The Death Penalty in America: Current Controversies.* 4th ed. New York: Oxford University Press, 1997.

Walter Berns — *For Capital Punishment: Crime and the Morality of the Death Penalty.* Lanham, MD: University Press of America, 1991.

Committee on the Judiciary — *Innocence and the Death Penalty: Assessing the Danger of Mistaken Executions.* Washington, DC: GPO, 1994.

Shirley Dicks, ed. — *Congregation of the Damned: Voices Against the Death Penalty.* Amherst, NY: Prometheus Books, 1991.

K.C. Haas and J.A. Inciardi, eds. — *Challenging Capital Punishment: Legal and Social Science Approaches.* Newbury Park, CA: Sage, 1988.

Enid Harlow et al., eds. — *The Machinery of Death: A Shocking Indictment of Capital Punishment in the United States.* New York: Amnesty International USA, 1995.

Jesse Jackson — *Legal Lynching: Racism, Injustice, and the Death Penalty.* New York: Marlowe, 1996.

Michael Kronenwetter — *Capital Punishment: A Reference Handbook.* Santa Barbara, CA: ABC-CLIO, 1993.

National Coalition to Abolish the Death Penalty — *The Death Penalty: The Religious Community Calls for Abolition.* Washington, DC: National Coalition to Abolish the Death Penalty, n.d.

Raymond Paternoster — *Capital Punishment in America.* New York: Lexington Books, 1991.

Helen Prejean — *Dead Man Walking: An Eyewitness Account of the Death Penalty in the United States.* New York: Random House, 1993.

Tracy L. Snell — *Bureau of Justice Statistics: Capital Punishment 1995.* Washington, DC: U.S. Department of Justice, Office of Justice Programs, 1997.

Mark V. Tushnet — *The Death Penalty.* New York: Facts On File, 1994.

Welsh S. White — *The Death Penalty in the Nineties.* Ann Arbor: University of Michigan Press, 1991.

Franklin E. Zimring and Gordon Hawkins   *Capital Punishment and the American Agenda.* New York: Cambridge University Press, 1986.

Periodicals

American Bar Association   "The Death Penalty: A Scholarly Forum," *Focus on Law Studies*, Spring 1997. Available from American Bar Association, 750 N. Lake Shore Dr., Chicago, IL 60611.

Hugo Adam Bedau   "The Case Against the Death Penalty," New York: American Civil Liberties Union, 1992. Available from Capital Punishment Project, ACLU, 122 Maryland Ave. NE, Washington, DC 20002.

Walter Berns and Joseph Bessette   "Why the Death Penalty Is Fair," *Wall Street Journal*, January 9, 1998.

Robert James Bidinotto   "The *Moral* Case for Capital Punishment," *LEAA Advocate*, Summer/Fall 1997. Available from Law Enforcement Alliance of America, 7700 Leesburg Pike, Suite 421, Falls Church, VA 22043.

Sharon Brownlee, Dan McGraw, and Jason Vest   "The Place for Vengeance," *U.S. News & World Report*, June 16, 1997.

David Cole   "Courting Capital Punishment," *Nation*, February 26, 1996.

John DiIulio   "Abolish the Death Penalty, Officially," *Wall Street Journal*, December 15, 1997.

Suzanne Donovan   "Shadow Figures: A Portrait of Life on Death Row," *Mother Jones*, July 29, 1997.

Economist   "Does the Death Penalty Deter Murder?" December 12, 1994.

Christopher Hitchens   "Scenes from an Execution," *Vanity Fair*, January 1998.

David A. Kaplan   "Life and Death Decisions," *Newsweek*, June 16, 1997.

John Kavanaugh   "Killing Persons, Killing Ethics," *America*, July 19, 1997.

Tom Kuntz and Anne Cronin   "The Rage to Kill Those Who Kill," *New York Times*, December 4, 1994.

Anthony Lewis   "Emotion, Not Reason," *New York Times*, January 2, 1998.

Peter Linebaugh   "The Farce of the Death Penalty," *Nation*, August 14–21, 1995.

Patrick V. Murphy   "Death Penalty Useless," *USA Today*, February 23, 1995.

Eric Pooley   "Death or Life?" *Time*, June 16, 1997.

Anna Quindlen   "The High Cost of Death," *New York Times*, November 19, 1994.

Eric Reitan — "Why the Deterrence Argument for Capital Punishment Fails," *Criminal Justice Ethics*, Winter 1993.

Lynn Scarlett — "Capital Punishment: No," *Reason*, June 1990.

Jacob Sullum — "Capital Punishment: Yes," *Reason*, June 1990.

Sam Howe Verhovek — "Across the U.S., Executions Are Neither Swift nor Cheap," *New York Times*, February 22, 1995.

Hiller Zobel — "The Undying Problem of the Death Penalty," *American Heritage*, December 1997.

Index